Arnold's
The Study of Poetry
A Critique

Arnold's
The Study of Poetry
A Critique

Matthew Arnold (1822-1888)

DR. RADHA MOHAN SINGH
Prof. & Head, Department of English
Patna University, Patna

DR. GUNJAN
Department of Functional English,
B.N. College, Patna University , Patna

MOTILAL BANARSIDASS PUBLISHERS
PRIVATE LIMITED • DELHI

First Edition: Delhi, ***2012***

ISBN: 978-81-208-3554-2

MOTILAL BANARSIDASS
41 U.A. Bungalow Road, Jawahar Nagar, Delhi 110 007
8 Mahalaxmi Chamber, 22 Bhulabhai Desai Road, Mumbai 400 026
203 Royapettah High Road, Mylapore, Chennai 600 004
236, 9th Main III Block, Jayanagar, Bangalore 560 011
Sanas Plaza, 1302 Baji Rao Road, Pune 411 002
8 Camac Street, Kolkata 700 017
Ashok Rajpath, Patna 800 004
Chowk, Varanasi 221 001

Printed in India
By Jainendra Prakash Jain at Shri Jainendra Press,
A-44, Naraina, Phase-I, New Delhi 110 028
and Published by Narendra Prakash Jain for
Motilal Banarsidass Publishers Private Limited,
Bungalow Road, Delhi 110 007

Dedicated to

All avid lovers of English criticism

Contents

Foreword

It was in 1902 that Herbert Paul eulogizing Arnold as a Critic wrote; 'No body' after reading "The Essays in Criticism" has any excuse for not being a critic. Ever since, the abiding import of Arnold's work has increasingly been realized and more and more universities have included *The Study of Poetry* in their syllabi. The present edition is an in-depth study of Arnold's *'The Study of Poetry'*. The book has been designed to fulfil the need of students. The relevant critical material has been presented in a lucid and simple manner. While the treatment is comprehensive and elaborate it in no way precludes a study of the original text which is a *sinequanon* for a proper and genuine understanding.

We are thankful to our respectful teachers for their constructive suggestions in preparing this book.

Thanks are due to Dr. S.B. Singh, T.M. University, Bhagalpur, Dr. S.M.P.N. Singh Sahi, Ranchi University, Dr. Binod Kumar Singh, Dr. Uday Shankar Ojha, J.P. University Chapra. Dr. A.K. Bachhan, Mithila University, Dr. Lalitesh Mishra, B.N. Mandal University, Dr. Saileshwar Sati Prasad, Prof. Sudha Thakur, Dr. Muniba Sami, Dr. Shankar Dutt, Dr. Shiv Jatan Thakur, Dr. Ila Sinha, Dr. C N Pandey, Dr. D.N. Sinha, Dr. S K Sharma, Dr. Stuti Prasad, Dr. Arjun Kumar,Dr Akhilesh Kumar Singh(Patna University) Dr. Bijoy Bahadur Singh, Dr. Arun Kumar, Dr. Saloni Kumar (College Of Commerce).

We are also grateful to our students Avinash, Ruby, Krishna Bhawani, Andaleeb Faridi, Lily, and all other students of Patna University.

We are also very thankful to Mr. A.K. Chaturvedi, the manager of Motilal Banarsidass, Patna branch without whose dynamic initiative, the book would not have seen the light of the day.

Finally, we must register our deep sense of gratitude to the publisher Motilal Banarsidass. We are very thankful to Mr. Ghulam Quadir who typed the manuscript neatly and meticulously without whom the book won't have been a reality.

Dr. Radha Mohan Singh
Gunjan

– 1 –

Introduction

(Matthew Arnold 1822-1888)

(a) THE MAN AND THE MOMENT

In one of his essays Arnold has observed that great literature is produced only when two factors coincide, the man and the moment, a man of natural ability and an age fertile in ideas. In a general way the formula is applicable to the case of Arnold himself because he was a representative intellectual of the Victorian age (1832-1900) and can be fully understood and appreciated only in the perspective of his times. It is, therefore, necessary to cast a brief glance at the *conditions prevailing in the Victorian age.*

The Victorian age in England was a period of rapid progress and unprecedented changes; and among the forces responsible for these upheavals only two deserve careful attention for our present purpose-scientific progress and the impact of the Industrial Revolution. The discoveries of science in its various branches were important not only materially and intellectually, but also religiously and spiritually. They were demolishing the very foundation of the religious faith, which rested on the infallibility of the Bible as the Divine Writ. We can illustrate the point with a couple of examples. Firstly, from time immemorial the Christian world tacitly accepted the history of the world as given in the Bible–that the world was created in six days by God, and was to live for six thousand years only, out of which four thousand years had already elapsed before the birth of Christ and the remaining tenure of the world's existence was not more than two thousand years. But the Victorian Geologists were discovering the shocking fact that the age of the earth and its term of existence were incalculable.

Secondly, Christianity, like other religions, had its own views about God, man and the future of humanity; that God was the creator and the sustainer of the universe which was moving according to his design; that God was not only almighty but also all-loving, He created man after His own image and placed the parents of mankind, 'Adam and Eve, in Eden, the garden of Paradise where they lived in a state of angelic purity an innocence for some time. But Satan, the fallen arch angel and enemy of God, assuming the form of a serpent, entered the happy garden and tempted Eve to taste the forbidden fruit in disobedience to the command of God, a cardinal sin in which Adam also became her partner or accomplice. The divine punishment came down like a bolt from the blue. Adam and Eve were expelled from Eden with the burden of hard toil and death and the original sin for themselves as well as their descendants, the generations of mankind. But out of His unquenchable love for man God sent down His own beloved Son, Christ, in the form of a frail human being to work, suffer and die upon the Cross so that his blood may wash away the sin of mankind and ensure the salvation of man. Ever since then the Christian baptism became a symbol of man's redemption and the entry of his soul into heaven. In the absence of this redeeming factor the soul remained tainted with sin and was destined ultimately to be consigned by God to the flame of the fiery hell, to undergo unending torture. Man, thus, was a strange creature, part animal and part divine, clothed in 'the muddy vesture of decay', but endowed, at the same time with a divine spark, an immortal soul which survives the decay and the death of the body. Among the discoveries of science the most explosive, in this respect, was the theory of Evolution, propounded by Darwin, in his two epoch-making works, The Origin of Species and The Descent of Man. The purport of Darwin's Theory may be given in a few words: the earth and the starry heavens were not created by a divine agency, but they have gradually evolved in the course of countless ages under the action and reaction of the natural forces. The universe was without purpose and the only law operating in the world of the living creatures was the survival of the fittest. Existence was a perpetual struggle to overcome the dangers presented by the environment, and in this struggle only those were calculated to survive who were the fittest, that is, the most cunning, resourceful and unscrupulous creatures. About the origin of the human soul, Wordsworth, the leader of the previous generation of poets, had proudly proclaimed in his 'Intimations of Immortality Ode':

Trailing clouds of glory do we come from God
And heaven lies around us in our infancy.

This is the essence of the old faith. But now Darwin was coolly showing that man has evolved from the monkey and there was no trustworthy evidence for any trace of immortality in him. He was the inhabitant of a tiny planet in a universe so vast indeed as to make his world an indistinct dot in the immensity of the celestial mechanism.

The tremendous impact of these theories can only be imagined. The feeling souls found suddenly that the solid ground on which they had stood with a sense of security had melted away, plunging them into the bog of incertitude and the polar light which was believed to have guided humanity through the ages suddenly went out leaving them dazed and groping for the way in darkness and in doubt. Tennyson, the representative poet of the age, was profoundly shaken and poured the anguish of his oppressed soul into his great elegy In Memoriam, occasioned by the death of his friend A.H. Hallam.

And Arnold described himself a wanderer between two worlds, the one dead and the other yet powerless to be born. The old world of faith and certitude was dead under the onslaughts of the scientific agnosticism and the birth of a new substitute for the old world was nowhere within sight. In this beautiful and popular lyric 'Dover Beach' he presents a vivid and feeling contrast between the old world of faith and the new scientific world of spiritual doubt, unrest and confusion. There was a time when the sea of Faith was full and lay clinging to the shores of the earth like a bright girdle round the waist. But now 'I only hear its melancholy, long withdrawing roar, retreating under the breath of the night winds from the rocky shores and the naked shingles of the earth'. The disappearance of faith has left the world, apparently so grand and beautiful, devoid of light, of certitude and of help for pain:

And we are here as on a darkling plain
Swept with the confused alarms of struggle and flight,
Where ignorant armies clash by night.

The world around him had really become 'a darkling plain', the field of Darwinian struggle for existence, a world of ruthless and cut-throat competition, when only those could survive and succeed who were unscrupulous, inhuman, resourceful and heartless. To a sensitive soul like Arnold it was, with all its external pomp and prosperity, a sick world, stricken with the strange disease of modern life 'its sick hurry and divided aims, its head overtaxed and its palsied heart'. In order to understand the nature of this sickness we must review the consequences of the Industrial Revolution in the contemporary English society. This revolution meant the introduction of machinery and construction of factories, of division of labour and large scale production. It also meant the sudden unemployment among the flourishing handicraftsmen and their gradual sinking into the slough of poverty, squalor and misery. There was a constant demand for labour which tempted millions of men and women from the countryside into the cities and towns which began to swell in size. The shift in population meant the break of village communities and the flooding of the industrial towns with men and women who had no other ties but economic interest. They were economic men and women, the factory hands, who worked as slaves tied to the iron machines, and came out of it utterly dehumanized to their tenements in the slums, the veritable homes of dirt, disease and darkness. Society witnessed the strange paradox of capitalism, the co-existence of plenty and poverty, plenty for the capitalists and poverty for the overworked millions, who for a long time were at the tender mercy of their masters. There was no trade union, no state protection and no human heart around to notice the cry of small, sleepy children in the noisy factories, who more often than not fell into the iron jaws of the machine which pulverized even their bones. The fast multiplication of wealth on the one hand and grim soul-killing poverty and drudgery on the other, were equally detrimental to culture, taste and regard for human values. Society was sinking into gross materialism where man was measured by the size of his purse and the worship of Mammon had replaced the worship of God, 'Render unto Caesar what belongs to Caesar and render unto me what belongs to me' was the famous demand of Christ, the embodiment of religious and spiritual values, and the Victorian Society was prepared only to deliver goods to Caesar, because Christ was no more a living inspiration. Arnold himself has clinched the nature of this society in a few telling words:

> *Our upper class is materialised, our middle-class vulgarised and our lower class brutalized.*

This was the condition of the age in which Arnold was placed by destiny to live, move and to act as an intellectual of enlightened mind, steeped in ancient and modern literatures, bent upon setting up as many posts of light in the growing darkness around him as it was possible for him to do. He was best fitted for the task because he was the son of Dr. Thomas Arnold, the great Headmaster of Rugby school; he was carefully educated and found his mind attuned to the magic of Oxford, the great seat of learning; by profession he was, for thirty-five years, an Inspector of schools, closely acquainted with the problems of education and doing his very best to inform the mind and refine the taste of the lower middle class, which he regarded as the sole repository of the critical taste in England.

But the crowning achievement of his career was his election to the chair of Professor of Poetry at Oxford University which he filled for ten years, without any detriment to his arduous duties as Inspector of schools. He was a poet, literary critic and the critic of the contemporary society, battling manfully with its immersion into the material concerns of life in order to propagate the best that has been thought and said, to spread the light and sweetness of the culture. This was a function of overwhelming importance because great poetry flourishes in an age capable of providing an order of ideas to feed and nourish the poetic genius. He was resolved to cultivate the soil proper for the growth of poetry because in the age of science when orthodox religion had become frozen and fossilized it was poetry which would fill the void and take over from religion the supreme function of consoling, elevating and tranquillizing the jaded minds of humanity, over-taxed by the growing complexity of life.

As we proceed to take a closer view of the literary works of Arnold we are struck with a division in his nature of which he himself was very well aware, and which has been fully supported as a trait common to most human beings, by the findings of modern psychology. In one of his less known poems "The Buried Life" Arnold speaks of two different selves of a human individual which may be described as public and private. The public self functions in the eye of his fellow men in the outer world, accepting their praise and blame as he contends with them for the prizes of life and shares the vicissitudes natural to that struggle. But behind this outer self, hidden in his depth beyond the reach of the inquisitive gaze of the world, there is his private self, genuine, instinctive and natural, untouched by the veneer of external culture and attainments. In terms of modern psychology the first is 'character' and the second is 'personality'.

The 'character' of Arnold is his prose self, representing the critic and the apostle of culture and reflecting the side of his self which forced itself in his youth on the attention of the people around him-the figure of a gay, oppish, cynical, witty, elegant youth who, with the sobriety of growing age cultivated 'Olympian growing manners' calm and unperturbed amid the tempests of life. This is the self that stood for objectivity, impersonality and universality in literature and found fault with the romantics for their lack of knowledge, excess of feeling and centrifugal tendencies and occasional lapses in taste and morality. But his real, private self which found expression in his poetry is romantic, shy, shivering and tender, looking back with wistful regret at the glories of the world buried in the bosom of the past.

(b) ARNOLD : THE POET

As a poet Arnold was essentially a romanticist, while as a critic he was professedly a classicist and defined poetry as 'a criticism of life under the laws of truth and beauty. He wrote a number of poems in conscious fulfilment of his critical creed, poems like *Empedocles on Etna, Merope, Sohrab and Rustam, Tristram and Iseult Balder Dead etc.* These poems, however, were still-born, and time has only thickened the layers of dust, settled on their leaves, and if Sohrab and Rustam has retained its popularity with the modern readers it is due not so much to its great action and inspiring message as to the pathos inherent in the fatal encounter of a warrior father with his heroic son, who stand face to face in utter ignorance, the truth of their kinship being revealed only when the fatal blow has fallen and the young son is lingering only on the brink of death.

It is true that much of Arnold's poetry is a criticism of life, but it is 'criticism' in a narrow, negative sense–a pensive probing into the heart of the mysterious disease of modern life, 'its sick hurry and divided aims'. He finds no consolation in nature and is too uncertain and unsettled in his attitude to offer any convincing interpretation of it. He is utterly helpless before the brutalities of real life, and magnifies this personal difference in his picture of humanity at large:

See! in the rocks of the world
Marches the host of mankind,
A feeble, wavering line!
Where are they tending?-A God
Marshall'd them, gave them their goal,
Ah, but the way is so long!

Such a poetry is ill-calculated to take the place of religion, and enlighten the mind, console the spirit and brace the nerves of our resolution. His nature, as revealed in his poetry, was essentially romantic, self-absorbed and introspective, but it was a romanticism, pale and drained of its blood and energy. He was a delicate representative of modern humanity, isolated alike from God and Nature, naked and shivering and brooding constantly on the deep wound of his heart which stands revealed in his verses. This explains the curious ambivalence in his attitude, to the great Romantics whom he criticises frankly but not without a secret longing for the spiritual wisdom of Wordsworth, the luminous wings of Shelley and the titanic energy of Byron, pitted against the laws of religion and morality.

Arnold is essentially a lyrical poet, though the singing garb sits loosely on his shoulders. The dominant strain in his lyricism is elegiac, which arises from the acute sense of loss, of something dear and valuable to us, either personally or as representatives of the human race. In his Scholar Gipsy, for example, the protagonist stands as a symbol of the happy past, when the mind was at peace, the wits were clear and 'life ran merrily like the sparkling Thames'. He is the norm against which the modern sick civilization, 'with its brain over-taxed and its palsied heart' is measured and judged. In the Dover Beach, as we have already mentioned, the sea-tide sounds the eternal note of sadness, reminding him of 'the melancholy, long, with drawing roar' of the retreating waters of Faith from the shores of the modern earth. The light of religion has departed, plunging the world into darkness, where races, like soldiers fighting in the darkness of the night, are engaged in political strife and commercial rivalries, where humanity does not count.

In his *Memorial Verses* and poems of kindred import he refers to individuals as symbols of human virtues and qualities which have departed with their deaths. Thus, the great German poet , Goethe, with his Olympian wisdom, is described as 'the physician of our Iron age; Wordsworth, the poet of nature, as the provider of the healing balm to the wounded heart of man, and Byron as a dynamo of titanic force, 'who taught us nothing', but was felt as 'thunders roll'. The glories of the world which once lent succour and consolation to man, are departed and man may now bank upon personal relationship for relief:

Only-but this is rare-
When a beloved hand is laid in ours,
When, jaded with the rush and glare
Of the interminable hours,
Our eyes can in another's eyes read clear,
When our world-deafened ear
Is by the tones of a loved voice caressed
A bolt is shot somewhere in our breast
A last pulse of feeling stirs again.

But his love poems, addressed to Marguerite, his lady love, poignantly point to the impossibility of such a union:

Yes! in the sea of life enisled,
With echoing straits between us thrown
Dotting the shoreless watery wild
We, mortal millions, live alone.

The lonely heart of the old romantics went to Nature for consolation and spiritual wisdom; Arnold also follows their track as a petitioner to the benign healer:

One lesson, Nature, let me learn of thee,
One lesson that in every wind is blown,
One lesson of two duties served in one-
Though the loud world proclaimed their enmity-
Of toil unsevered from transquility.

But Nature does not respond and seems to rebuke him for harbouring a restless fever in his heart :

Hast thou, then, still, the old unquiet breast,
Which neither deadens into rest
Nor even feels the fiery glow
That whirls the spirit from itself away.
But fluctuates to and fro,
Never by passion quite possessed,
And never quite benumbed by the world's show.

Arnold is the poet of loveliness par excellence, and all his protagonists are lonely figures; his Scholar Gipsy is a lonely seeker after 'fugitive and gracious light', clutching the inviolable shade of the forest beyond the access of the modern diseased humanity:

Out of the heed of mortals he is gone,
He wends unfollow'd, he must house alone,
Yet on he fares, by his own heart inspired

His picture of Shakespeare also is that of a lonely Titan, standing all alone, 'self-school'd, self-scann'd, self-honour'd, self-secure'

But lacking the strength and self-possession of such heroes and with the unquenched fever still burning in his heart, Arnold gives way to a Hamlet-like feeling of world-weariness, when life becomes an unbearable burden:

We cannot kindle when we Will
The fire which in our heart resides;
The spirit bloweth and is still
In mystery our soul abides-
With aching hands and bleeding feet
We dig and heap, lay stone on stone:
We bear the burden and the heat
Of the long day, and wish 't' were done'.

He sometime uses the image of sea-voyage or uphill journey to signify the collective effort of mankind for moral progress, yet in both the cases storm and thunder crash are quite on the card and only a few way-farers can escape disaster and death. They reach the goal, broken and alone:

We bring
Only ourselves! We lost
Sight of the rest in the storm!
Friends, companions and trains
The avalanche swept from our side.

The only remedy lies in fatalism, the last refuge for helpless mortals, who unable to take up the sword against a sea of troubles, have to sweat and grunt under the burden of life.

...and we others pine,
And wish the long unhappy dream would end,
And waive all claims to bliss, and try to bear.

With close-lipped patience for our only friend,
Sad patience, too near neighbour to despair.

But what is remarkable with Arnold's pessimism in his suavity, the sweetness which rises out of his bitterness and suffuses the whole poem.

Thus, the spirit of Arnold's poetry is subdued romanticism, the keynote of which is a tender wistful melancholy. But the form and style of his poems are classical, with occasional infusion of romantic richness in phrasing and single passages. He follows the classical ideal of simplicity, directness and lucidity, and scrupulously avoids exuberance of diction and imagery. His poetry has generally the qualities of good prose, where each word has weight and no word is superfluous. Apart from this verbal precision there is his intellectual control of the material which contributes to the architectural design of the poem and the logical evolution of thought. He is not a spontaneous singer: he has neither wings, nor fire he can neither stir our heart nor kindle our nerves. He is a cultured mediator, sweet in his sadness and moving in his pensive meditativeness and will always have his peculiar appeal to the sensitive readers. His poetic vein was soon exhausted. Some say that poetry was willingly abandoned in favour of the prose criticism and propaganda to make society worthy of great poetry; while others have categorically stated that his strong intellectualism extinguished the poetic spark in his soul. Middleton Murry has argued in favour of inner conflict as the main cause of Arnold's; poetic exhaustion: 'In Matthew Arnold, the poet, there were two men, who struggled with one another till they were both exhausted, and the poet was dead. We may call one of these romantic and the other classical; or we may say that one was the heart and the other the head'.

(c) ARNOLD : THE CRITIC

Arnold's criticism, literary, social and religious, represents his determined and inspired endeavour to combat the forces operative in society, which, as a poet, he viewed and commented upon in a spirit of helpless, pensive melancholy. At the back of his mind was the image of the heroes of forlorn causes who wage a careless war with the odds around them till they fall down broken but unbent. One is reminded here of his closing words in the essay on Byron:

"As the inevitable break-up of the old order comes, as the English middle class slowly awakens from its intellectual sleep of two centuries, as our actual present world to which this sleep has condemned us, shows itself more clearly-our world of an aristocracy materialised and rank, a middle class purblind and hideous, a lower class crude and brutal–we shall turn our eyes again, and to more purpose, upon this passionate and dauntless soldier of a forlorn hope, who, ignorant of the future, and unconsoled by its promises, nevertheless, waged against the conservation of the old impossible -world a fiery battle, waged it till he fell-waged it with such splendid and imperishable excellence of sincerity and strength."

The vision of the future set-up which prompted the critical efforts of Arnold was that of a society in which the function of religion, the function of consoling, tranquillising and elevating the mind of man by giving him an insight into the beauty, dignity and nobility of human life, has been taken up by poetry. But poetry to be able to take up this grand office must be built on sound principles and must flourish in a society replete with ideas and the free play of the mind. The mission of creating social conditions favorable for the birth, growth and expansion of the new poetry was assigned by him to the critics of art and literature. Thus there runs a continuous thread of unity through all the critical works of Arnold, which are specified below:

The *Preface to the Poems* (1853) where Arnold outlines the nature of the new classical poetry, deliberately in opposition to the romantic poetry his age had inherited. Then came his Oxford lecture, *On Translating Homer* (1861) which expounds the qualities of the grand style to be the vehicle of the new poetry. The next course of lectures, *On the Study of Celtic Literature (1867)*, an excursion into the domain of primitive poetry. His articles and miscellaneous essays were collected and published in three series, under the title, *Essays in Criticism,* first series (1865); second series (1888) and third series after his death (in 1910). These essays deal mainly with the poets, continental and English, and reveal his strength and limitations as a literary critic. Among his essays in social criticism the most significant is *Culture and Anarchy (1869)*, a detailed and impassioned plea for that cultural perfection which may make English society worthy of great poetry, at once its progeny and its spiritual nurse.

The poetic reform suggested by Arnold implies negatively a rejection of the romantic ideals and positively an adoption of the ideals of the classical Greece, represented by Homer and Sophocles. His criticism of the Romantic Movement in English poetry of the early 19th century is directed against its *subjectivism:* it is an allegory of the poet's own mind; its *emotionalism:* the romantic poets, he says, belong to the movement of feeling rather than to the movement of thought: and its isolation from the main currents of the modern age. They did not know enough, for they willfully, turned their backs upon the multiplication of knowledge, which followed in the wake of the rapid developments in science.

Moreover, the Romantic poetry seems to be inclined to prefer rich fragments to the well-built whole; it lacks *ordomance* or architectonic. Lastly, the style of Romantic poetry is marked by exuberance by the pomp and prodigality of diction and wealth of images and ornamentation out of all proportion to the idea, they-are intended to express or elucidate.

The new poetry based on the practice of the Hellenic (pure Greek) poets is anatomised in the 1853 *Preface* which deserves a brief examination:

(i) The poet, in the first place, has to select an excellent action; and what actions are the most excellent? Those certainly, which most powerfully appeal to the great primary human affections: to those elementary feelings which subsist permanent in the race and which are independent of time. The modernness or antiquity of an action has nothing to do with its fitness for poetical representation; this depends on its inherent qualities.

(ii) The second quality in which the Greek practice is diametrically opposed to that of modern poets may be described in a nut-shell by saying that they thought of the whole, while we think in terms of brilliant fragments and purple patches. 'We have poems which seem to exist for the sake of single lines and passages; not for the sake of producing any total impression. The example for this unfortunately was set by great Shakespeare himself, who added to his eminent qualities 'a gift of happy, abundant, ingenious expression, eminent and unrivalled; so eminent as irresistibly to strike the attention first in him, and even to throw into comparative shade his other excellences as a poet. He has been the mischief.' Arnold therefore, recommends that after the choice of the great action the poet should proceed to arrange its various parts in such a way as to produce the sense of a whole with its various parts mutually bound together and each contributing to the effect of the whole in proportion to its importance in the design. This is a quality which is technically known as the 'architectonic'–a quality which Goethe has described as the distinguishing mark of a genuine artist. Arnold defines it as 'that power of execution, which creates, forms and executes: not the profoundness of single thoughts, not the richness of imagery, not the abundance of illustration.

So, the qualities which the modern poets, desirous of producing great poetry, may learn from the ancients are the 'all-importance of the choice of a subject; the necessity of accurate construction, and the subordinate character of the expression'.

(iii) It means that the style should be only a means to an end, perfectly adapted to the subject and willingly subservient to its purpose and never trying to claim attention beyond its moderate limit, this perfect style, of which the ancients were the supreme masters, has been termed by Arnold 'the grand style', which he discusses at length in his *On Translating Homer.* Grand style, he says there, 'arises in poetry when a noble nature poetically gifted, treats with simplicity or severity a serious subject'. Of grand style sample the model is Homer; of grand style severe the best exemplar is Milton, while in Dante the two aspects are blended together. The whole discussion is unhappily worded, but the intention of the critic is quite clear. By grand style he simply signifies the classical or Attic style, simple, precise, restrained, lucid, pregnant and scrupulously denuded of all show and unnecessary ornamentation. This style was anciently opposed to the Asiatic style, which, for Arnold, was best represented by the Romantics. An old critic has put the distinction between the two in a telling analogy-the Attic is the modest bride, and the Asiatic is the meretricious harlot.

(iv) The 'Preface' glances at Aristotle's view of poetry as the imitation or representation of life. But mere representation, however accurate it may be, is not enough, it has to be shown also that it is a representation from which men can derive enjoyment. In presence of the most tragic circumstances, represented in a work of art, the feeling of enjoyment, as is well known, may still subsist: the representation of the most utter calamity, of the liveliest anguish, is not sufficient to destroy it: the more tragic the situation, the deeper becomes the enjoyment, and the situation is more tragic in proportion as it becomes more terrible. A representation to be poetical must inspirit and rejoice the reader: it must convey a charm and infuse delight. For, the Muses, as Heriod says, were born that they might be 'a forgetfulness of evils and a truce from cares', "All Art", says Schiller, 'is dedicated to Joy, and there is no higher and no more serious problem than how to make men happy. The right Art is that alone, which creates the highest enjoyment'.

(v) Further analysis of the nature of great poetry is taken up in 'the Study of Poetry', one of the most crucial critical essays by Arnold. The best poetry, he says, will be found to have a power of forming, sustaining and delighting us as nothing else can. If poetry is to fulfill its high destinies it must be 'a criticism of life under the conditions fixed for such a criticism by the laws of poetic truth and poetic beauty', It means that the truth about life implicit in the poetic representation of it must be productive of delight by virtue of the charm infused into it by the art of poetry.

(vi) But delightful truth of life implicit in the poetic representation is not, in itself enough to constitute the greatness and excellence of poetry. Poetry to be really great must be a grand application of ideas to life, to the great question of how to live; and it must possess high seriousness. Thus two additional qualifications have been added to the conception of poetry as the criticism of life. The poet must represent life in such a way as to make it illustrative of certain noble ideas which may console, sustain and inspire the readers. Such ideas may relate to the beauty and glory of life despite evil and suffering which are mingled in its tissue; and also the greatness and dignity of man, the spiritual strength that is hidden in his frail body, and the high aspirations of his soul with all the frailties of his flesh. These ideas were formerly supplied by religion, which has now become discredited as a fact, but its ideas may be taken over and remitted by poetry to pass among modern men and women as a valid currency. Eliot has well said that if man were to be stripped of all the attributes which religion has invested him with, he will certainly be no better than a naked, weak and pernicious animal. 'High seriousness' of poetry means a representation of life, poetically conceived and providing a clear insight into the depth of life below its superficialities, varieties and contradictions. This depth is the repository of all the primary affections and elementary passions which are universal and permanent, common to the members of the race in all climes and periods of history. Poetry which represents these will have a universal appeal and may foster the sense of affinity and brotherhood and thereby fulfil its high mission, which in the words of Wordsworth, is to bind together, with knowledge and passion the vast empire of mankind.

This high seriousness' implies sincerity, the force of conviction, the sense that the poetic representation contains a truth which rises from the depth of the poet's heart and has the power to penetrate the heart of the reader.

(vii) In the essay on Wordsworth Arnold odds one more attribute. He refers to Voltaire's remark about English poets who have distinguished themselves by the treatment of moral ideas with energy and depth, the term 'moral' in a general and broad sense is an integral part of life and consequently, 'a poetry of revolt against moral ideas is a poetry of revolt against life; a poetry of indifference towards moral ideas is a poetry of indifference towards life.

(viii) It is not necessary to describe in abstract terms the best way of discovering the excellence of a poem, because there can be no more useful help for discovering what poetry belong to the class of the truly excellent and can, therefore, do us most good, than to have always in one's mind lines and expressions of the great masters and to apply them as a touch stone to other poetry. Lines from Homer, Dante, Shakespeare and Milton and other poets whose excellence and eminence have been accepted by readers of all countries and times.

(d) THE NATURE OF HIS CRITICISM AND ITS LIMITATIONS

This, in brief, is Arnold's idea of great poetry which, with the progress of science and sophistication will become more and more the mainstay of mankind for that joy, consolation and uplift of man's mind and soul which were previously afforded by religion. From this it is not difficult to understand that Arnold belongs to the class of those critics, who, may properly be described as Platonist that is critics who like Plato, the great Greek philosopher and the first eminent critic of art and letters, consider poetry in relation to life. Poetry must contribute to the moral and spiritual development of the readers; cultivate in them qualities requisite for fashioning a good citizen, healthy, balanced and discriminating, loving virtues and abhorring vices of all kinds. Certain consequences follow from such a conception of poetry, which are regarded as limitations in the critic of this school:

(i) A critic of this school of which Arnold is a known type of inapt to examine poetry as poetry, to consider it as an art; to analyse the various parts and components of a poem, its diction and imagery, for disentangling its peculiar flavour. Eliot has said that Arnold was a propagandist for criticism rather than a true critic, he has talked much about the duty of a critic as the zealous propagator of the best that has been thought and said in the world in order to create an atmosphere in society for the birth and progress of great poetry, but he has not cared to promote the reader's understanding and enjoyment of a poem through analysis and comparison. The 'touch stone' method suggested by him is not helpful in this respect because what is excellent to one critic may not be the same for another.

(ii) In judging the various poets Arnold applies one uniform standard of great poetry which is already present in his mind; and the application is indiscriminate, as it makes no distinction between one poet and another, and at times, militates against that 'disinterestedness' which he himself described as a valuable requisite of a good critic. Thus, Chaucer and Burns are slighted for lacking 'high seriousness'; Shelley for the absence of substance in his poetry, which makes him a beautiful and ineffectual angel, beating in the void his luminous wings in vain.

(iii) As poetry is considered in relation to life, it is easy for the critic to pass from the poetry of a writer to his life and colour his criticism with a prejudice born of the life and character of the author as a man.

Illustrations of this fact are afforded by his sharp reactions to Shelley's infidelity to his first wife, and John Keats' unhealthy self-abandonment to morbid cravings and yearnings which the consumptive, dying young poet poured into his love letters addressed to Fanny Browne, his lady love.

(iv) Arnold recommended disinterestedness and objectivity as qualities which a critic must cultivate, together with a peculiar temper of mind, which sees the thing as it really is and never suffers the mind to be perverted by 'personal, national, provincial or doctrinal prejudice'. But his own criticism and estimates of poets are occasionally vitiated by partiality, prejudice and dogmatism. Thus, he underrates Shelly and over rates Byron; lavishes high praise on Gray but ignores Collins, and in his critical excursions on continental poets he dwells on a number of minor figures whose memory is preserved only in his pages.

The same limitation is apparent in the brief historical sketch of the progress of English poetry. He does not even mention Donne and the Metaphysical poets.

(v) Arnold manifestly lacks one other important attribute of a great critic-namely, precise critical terminology employed in his discussions and expositions. In his definition of poetry he uses terms and phrases - 'interpretation of life'; 'criticism of life' and 'grand application of ideas to life' - which are vague and ambiguous. Similar is the case with the phrase 'high seriousness' attributed to high poetry, which he repeats but does not explain in clear terms. His conception of 'grand style' is similarly vague because he defines it generally, briefly and we may say, faultily, because he would have us believe that 'simplicity' and 'severity' are antithetical and mutually exclusive terms.

(e) HIS PLACE IN THE HISTORY OF CRITICISM

In spite of his many and serious limitations no student of English literature can question his eminence as a critic and the tremendous influence he exerted on the subsequent developments of criticism in England. In an age of scientific intellectualism and growing debasement of taste in art and literature he pleaded vehemently for the creation, cultivation and perusal of great poetry which alone can save the soul of humanity in an age of agnosticism and religious decline. His conception of poetry was high and noble and his missionary zeal for the preservation of the poetic and critical values is still a living inspiration for all the apologists of poetry in our iconoclastic and nihilistic age. Even T.S. Eliot, his worst critic, and I.A. Richards, the two pillars of criticism in the present century, are in direct line of descent from Arnold and represent his moralistic approach, based on the social value of poetry.

Secondly, Arnold's bitter criticism of insularity of taste in England and his repeated emphasis on the necessity of regarding the culture of the whole Europe as a single unit, and the literature of a particular nation as a part of the European literature, found its most elaborate statement at the hands of T.S. Eliot in his first important critical essay, 'Tradition and Individual Talent', where the literary tradition is defined as the literature of entire Europe from the age of Homer down to this day, and within it the whole of one's national literature from its beginning to the present moment.

Thirdly, the method of comparative criticism, implying comparison between native and continental writers, as well as the necessity of European recognition as a mark of a poet's real greatness, which are apparent in Arnold's criticism, handsomely anticipate an important critical trend in modern criticism.

Equally fruitful and modern is his opposition to the romantic ideas in poetry, and commendation of objectivity, impersonality, universality and structural unity, which became the criteria of the new poetry which Pound and Eliot succeeded in building in the second decade of the present century. He is modern again in his insistence upon the necessity of due recognition, on the part of poets, of the growing complexity and multiplicity of knowledge which science has piled up in the course of its rapid developments. Arnold's eminence as a critic lies not so much in his power of analysis and exposition of the individual poets and poems, as in the valuable service he rendered to his age as a trustworthy guide in a period of critical confusion. The great romantic movement had declined by the time of his critical debut and a new approach to poetry was the crying need of the hour. In the establishment of this new approach no critic was as effective and competent as Arnold. In this respect it is pertinent to recall the memorable estimate of T.S. Eliot who was otherwise disposed to disparage Arnold, the critic:

"From time to time every hundred years or so it is desirable that some critic shall appear to review the past of our literature and set the poets and the poems in the new order. This task has been performed by Dryden, Johnson, Arnold, as well as human frailty could allow. This task of new assignment is necessary because no generation is interested in Art in quite the same way as any other."

It was desirable after the surprising, varied and abundant contribution of the romantic period that this task of criticism should be taken up again. Nothing that was done in this period was of the nature of what Arnold was able to do, because that was not the time in which it could be done... He was an educator, the valuation of Romantic poets, in academic circles, is still very largely that which Arnold made. It was right, it was just, it was necessary for its time: and of course it had its defects. His intrinsic qualities as a critic can be summed up in the words of Prof. Saintsbury:

"Systematic without being hide-bound; well read (without being exactly learned) without pedantry delicate and subtle, without weakness or dilettantism; Catholic without eclecticism; enthusiastic without indiscriminateness - Mr. Arnold is one of the best and most precious of teachers on his own side."

ARNOLD'S PROSE STYLE

In "The Study of Poetry' while commenting on the eighteenth century, the age of prose, Arnold observes, the needful qualities of a fit prose are regularity, uniformity, precision, balance'. All these (with lucidity which Arnold does not mention) are the qualities of classical prose, of which Arnold is one of the best exemplars. He handles it in his own way and gives it the stamp of his personality with its strength and limitation. His prose is critical, but deals with diverse themes of poetic and social significance. This gives it considerable flexibility. It may be regular and grave, witty and conversational; it may abound in felicities of expression as in the essays on Keats, Wordsworth and Shelley, but it may also touch the point of eloquence as in the closing paragraphs in the essay on Byron.

Lucidity is the principal quality which determines the main features of this prose and the choice of words, use of figures and images as well as the cast of sentences are determined by it. Precision in the choice of words is a basic quality, in the observance of which Arnold is not free from occasional lapses. Some of his words and phrases 'Poetry is the criticism of life; grand application of ideas to life; high seriousness, grand style have become current in literature and are often repeated by his students but they are not free from ambiguity. On the whole, however, his -arguments are lucid; logically regulated in sentences of moderate length and his apparently long sentences are usually a series of short clauses, each complete in itself. This reliance upon loose structure betokens an apparent lack of system and carefully-built structure. It has been construed by Eliot as a sign of mental limitation. It shows, says Eliot, 'that Arnold was lacking in the power of connected reasoning at any length. His flights are either short flights or circular flights'. But the whole essay entitled 'Culture and Anarchy' is an example of sustained flight and uniform excellence.

One great quality of Arnold the prose writer is his power to throw up a number of striking sentences, pregnant and pithy and therefore, memorable and quotable. His 'Study of Poetry' alone can furnish at least half a dozen good examples. Arnold is not free from lapses and mannerisms, but at its best his prose is marked by intellectual energy and subdued fire of passion which show that the man speaking is serious of purpose and anxious to carry his convictions home to his readers.

– 2 –

The Study of Poetry

(a) TEXT

'The future of poetry is immense, because in poetry, where it is worthy of its high destinies, our race, as time goes on, will find an ever surer and surer stay. There is not a creed which is not shaken, not an accredited dogma which is not shown to be questionable, not a received tradition which does not threaten to dissolve. Our religion has materialised itself in the fact, in the supposed fact; it has attached its emotion to the fact, and now the fact is failing it. But for poetry the idea is everything; the rest is a world of illusion, of divine illusion. Poetry attaches its emotion to the idea; the idea is the fact. The strongest part of our religion today is its unconscious poetry."

Let me be permitted to quote these words of my own, as uttering the thought which should, in my opinion, go with us and govern us in all our study of poetry. In the present work it is the course of one great contributory stream to the world - river of poetry that we are invited to follow. We are here invited to trace the stream of English poetry. But whether we set ourselves, as here, to follow only one of the several streams that make the mighty river of poetry, or whether we seek to know them all, our governing thought should be the same. We should conceive of poetry worthily, and more highly than it has been the custom to conceive of it. We should conceive of it as capable of higher uses, and called to higher destinies, than those which in general men have assigned to it hitherto. More and more mankind will discover that we have to turn to poetry to interpret life for us, to console us, to sustain us. Without poetry, our science will appear incomplete; and most of what now passes with us for religion and philosophy will be replaced by poetry. Science, I say, will appear incomplete without it. For finely and truly does Wordsworth call poetry 'the impassioned expression which is in the countenance of all science'; and what is a countenance without its expression? Again, Wordsworth finely and truly calls poetry 'the breath and finer spirit of all knowledge'; our religion, parading evidences such as those on which the popular mind relies now; our philosophy, pluming itself on its reasoning about causation and finite and infinite being; what are they but the shadows and dreams and false shows of knowledge? The day will come when we shall wonder at ourselves for having trusted to them, for having taken them seriously; and the more we perceive their hollowness, the more we shall prize 'the breath and finer spirit of knowledge' offered to us by poetry.

But if we conceive thus highly of the destinies of poetry, we must also set our standard for poetry high, since poetry, to be capable of fulfilling such high destinies, must be poetry of a high order of excellence. We must accustom ourselves to a high standard and to a strict judgment. Sainte - Beuve relates that Napoleon one day said, when somebody was spoken of in his presence as a charlatan: 'Charlatan as much as you please; but where is there *not* charlatanism? - 'Yes', answers Sainte - Beuve, 'in politics, in the art of governing mankind, that is perhaps true, But in the order of thought, in art, the glory, the eternal honour is that charlatanism shall find no entrance; herein lies the inviolableness of that noble portion of man's being. It is admirably said, and let us hold fast to it. In poetry, which is thought and art in one, it is the glory, the eternal honour, that charlatanism shall find no entrance; that this noble sphere be kept inviolate and inviolable. Charlatanism is for confusing or obliterating the distinctions between excellent and inferior, sound and unsound or only half - sound, true and untrue or only half - true. It is charlatanism, conscious or unconscious, whenever we confuse or obliterate these. And in poetry, more than anywhere else, it is impermissible to confuse or obliterate them. For in poetry the distinction between excellent and inferior, sound and unsound or only half - sound, true and untrue or only half - true, is of paramount importance. It is of paramount importance because of the high destinies of poetry. In poetry, as a criticism of life under the conditions fixed for such a criticism by the laws of poetic truth and poetic beauty, the spirit of our race will find, we have said,. as time goes on and as other helps fail, its consolation and stay. But the consolation and stay will be of power in proportion to the power of the criticism of life. And the criticism of life will be of power in proportion as the poetry conveying it is excellent rather than inferior, sound rather than unsound or half - sound, true rather than untrue on half - true.

The best poetry is what we want; the best poetry will be found to have a power of forming, sustaining, and delighting us, as nothing else can. A clearer, deeper sense of the best in poetry, and of the strength and joy to be drawn from it, is the most precious benefit which we can gather from a poetical collection such as the present. And yet in the very nature and conduct of such a collection there is inevitably something which tends to obscure in us the consciousness of what our benefit should be, and to distract us from the pursuit of it. We should therefore steadily set it before our minds at the outset, and should compel ourselves to revert constantly to the thought of it as we proceed.

Yes; constantly in reading poetry, a sense for the best, the really excellent, and of the strength and joy to be drawn from it, should be present in our minds and should govern our estimate of what we read. But this real estimate, the only true one, is liable to be superseded, if we are not watchful, by two other kinds of estimates, the historic estimate and the personal estimate, both of which are fallacious. A poet or a poem may count to us historically, they may count to us on grounds personal to ourselves, and they may count to us really. They may count to us historically. The course of development of a nation's language, thought, and poetry, is profoundly interesting; and by regarding a poet's work as a stage in this course of development we may easily bring ourselves to make it of more importance as poetry than in itself it really is, we may come to use a language of quite exaggerated praise in criticising it; in short, to over - rate it. So arises in our poetic judgments the fallacy caused by the estimate which we may call historic. Then, again, a poet or poem may count to us on grounds personal to ourselves. Our personal affinities, likings and circumstances, have great power to sway our estimate of this or that poet's work, and to make us attach more importance to it as poetry than in itself it really possesses, because to us it is, or has been, of high importance. Here also we over - rate the object of our interest, and apply to it a language of praise which is quite exaggerated. And thus we get the source of a second fallacy in our poetic judgments - the fallacy caused by an estimate which we may call personal.

Both fallacies are natural. It is evident how naturally the study of the history and development of a poetry may incline a man to pause over reputations and works once conspicuous but now obscure, and to quarrel with a careless public for skipping, in obedience to mere tradition and habit, from one famous name or work in its national poetry to another, ignorant of what it misses, and of the reason for keeping what it keeps, and of the whole process of growth in its poetry. The French have become diligent students of their own early poetry, which they long neglected; the study makes many of them dissatisfied with their so - called classical poetry, the court - tragedy of the seventeenth century, a poetry which Pellisson long ago reproached with its want of the true poetic stamp, with its *politesse sterile et rampant*, but which nevertheless has reigned in France as absolutely as if it had been the perfection of classical poetry indeed. The dissatisfaction is natural; yet a lively and accomplished critic, M. Charles d' Héricault, the editor of Clement Marot, goes too far when he says that 'the cloud of glory playing round a classic is a mist as dangerous to the future of a literature as it is intolerable for the purposes of history. 'It hinders', he goes on, 'it hinders us from seeing more than one single point, the culminating and exceptional point; the summary, fictitious and arbitrary, of a thought and of a work. It substitutes a halo for a physiognomy, it puts a statue where there was once a man, and hiding from us all trace of the labour, the attempts, the weaknesses, the failures, it claims not study but veneration; it does not show us how the thing is done, it imposes upon us a model. Above all, for the historian this creation of classic personages is inadmissible; for it withdraws the poet from his time, from his proper life, it breaks historical relationships, it blinds criticism by conventional admiration, and renders the investigation of literary origins unacceptable. It gives us a human personage no longer but a God seated immovable amidst His perfect work, like Jupiter on Olympus; and hardly will it be possible for the young student to whom such work is exhibited at such a distance from him, to believe that it did not issue ready - made from that divine head.

All this is brilliantly and tellingly said, but we must plead for a distinction. Everything depends on the reality of a poet's classic character. If he is a dubious classic, let us sift him; if he is a false classic, let us explode him. But if he is a real classic, if his work belongs to the class of the very best (for this is the true and right meaning of the word classic, classical), then the great thing for us is to feel and enjoy his work as deeply as ever we can, and to appreciate the wide difference between it and all work which has not the same high character. This is what is salutary, this is what is formative; this is the great benefit to be got from the study of poetry. Everything which interferes with it, which hinders it, is injurious. True, we must read our classic with open eyes, and not with eyes blinded with superstition; we must perceive when his work comes short, when it drops out of the class of the very best, and we must rate it, in such cases, at its proper value. But the use of this negative criticism is not in itself, it is entirely in its enabling us to have a clearer sense and a deeper enjoyment of what is truly excellent. To trace the labour, the attempts, the weaknesses, the failures of a genuine classic, to acquaint oneself with his time and his life and his historical relationships, is mere literary dilettantism unless it has that clear sense and deeper enjoyment for its end. It may be said that the more we know about a classic the better we shall enjoy him; and, if we lived as long as Methuselah and had all of us heads of perfect clearness and wills of perfect steadfastness, this might be true in fact as it is plausible in theory. But the case here is much the same as the case with the Greek and Latin studies of our schoolboys. The elaborate philological groundwork which we require them to lay is in theory an admirable preparation for appreciating the Greek and Latin authors worthily. The more thoroughly we lay the groundwork, the better we shall be able, it may be said, to enjoy the authors. True, if time were not so short, and schoolboys' wits not so soon tired and their power of attention exhausted; only, as it is, the elaborate philological preparation goes on, but the authors are little known and less enjoyed. So with the investigator of 'historic origins' in poetry. He ought to enjoy the true classic all the better for his investigations; he often is distracted from the enjoyment of the best, and with the less good he over busies himself, and is prone to over - rate it in proportion to the trouble which it has cost him.

The idea of tracing historic origins and historical relationships cannot be absent from a compilation like the present. And naturally the poets to be exhibited in it will be assigned to those persons for exhibition who are known to prize them highly, rather than to those who have no special inclination towards them. Moreover, the very occupation with an author, and the business of exhibiting him, disposes us to affirm and amplify his importance. In the present work, therefore, we are sure of frequent temptation to adopt the historic estimate, or the personal estimate, and to forget the real estimate; which latter, nevertheless, we must employ if we are to make poetry yield us its full benefit. So high is that benefit, the benefit of clearly feeling and of deeply enjoying the really excellent, the truly classic in poetry, that we do well, I say, to set it fixedly before our minds as our object in studying poets and poetry, and to make the desire of attaining it the one principle to which, as the Imitation says, whatever we may read or come to know, we always return. *Cum multa legeris et cognoveris, ad unum semper oportet redire principium.*

The historic estimate is likely in especial to affect our judgment and our language when we are dealing with ancient poets; the personal estimate when we are dealing with poets our contemporaries, or at any rate modern. The exaggerations due to the historic estimate are not in themselves, perhaps, of very much gravity. Their report hardly enters the general ear; probably they do not always impose even on the literary men who adopt them. But they lead to a dangerous abuse of language. So we hear Caedmon, amongst our own poets, compared to Milton. I have already noticed the enthusiasm of one accomplished French critic for 'historic origins'. Another eminent French critic, M. Vitet, comments upon that famous document of the early poetry of his nation, the *Chanson de Roland.* It is indeed a most interesting document. The joculator or jongleur Taillefer, who was with William the Conqueror's army at Hastings, marched before the Norman troops, so said the tradition, singing' of Charlemagne and of Roland and of Oliver, and of the vassals who died at Roncevaux'; and it is suggested that in the Chanson de Roland by one Turoldus or Theroulde, a poem preserved in a manuscript of the twelfth century in the Bodleian Library at Oxford, we have certainly the matter, perhaps even some of the words, of the chant which Taillefer sang. The poem has vigour and freshness; it is not without pathos. But M. Vitet is not satisfied with seeing in it a document of some poetic value, and of very high historic and linguistic value; he sees in it a grand and beautiful work, a monument of epic genius. In its general design he finds the grandiose conception, in its details he finds the constant union of simplicity with greatness, which are the marks, he truly says, of the genuine epic, and distinguish it from the artificial epic of literary ages. One thinks of Homer; this is the sort of praise which is given to Homer, and justly given. Higher praise there cannot well be, and it is the praise due to epic poetry of the highest order only, and to no other. Let us try, then, the *Chanson de Roland* at its best. Roland, mortally wounded, lay himself down under a pine - tree, with his face turned towards Spain and the enemy -

De plusurs choses a remembrer li prist,
De tantes teres cume li bers cunquist,
De dulce France, des humes de sun lign,
De Carlemagne sun seignor ki l'nurrit.

That is primitive work, I repeat, with an undeniable poetic quality of its own. It deserves such praise, and such praise is sufficient for it. But now turn to Homer: - 'So said she; they long since in Earth's soft arms were reposing, There, in their own dear land, their fatherland, Lacedaemon.' - Iliad,' iii. 243, 244 (translated by Dr. Hawtrey).

We are here in another world, another order of poetry altogether; here is rightly due such supreme praise as that which M. Vitet gives to the Chanson de Roland. If our words are to have any meaning, if our judgments are to have any solidity, we must not heap that supreme praise upon poetry of an order immeasurably inferior.

Indeed there can be no more useful help for discovering what poetry belongs to the class of the truly excellent, and can therefore do us most good, than to have always in one's mind lines and expressions of the great masters, and to apply them as a touchstone to other poetry. Of course we are not to require this other poetry to resemble them; it may be very dissimilar. But if we have any tact we shall find them, when we have lodged them well in our minds, infallible touchstone for detecting the presence or absence of high poetic quality, and also the degree of this quality, in all other poetry which we may place beside them. Short passages, even single lines, will serve our turn quite sufficiently. Take the two lines which I have just quoted from Homer, the poet's comment on Helen's mention of her brothers; - or take his'Ah, unhappy pair, why gave we you to King Peleus, to a mortal? but ye are without old age, and immortal. Was it that with men born to misery ye might have sorrow?' - 'Iliad,' xvii.443-445. the address of Zeus to the horses of Peleus; - or take finally his 'Nay, and thou too, old man, in former days wast, as we hear, happy.' - 'Iliad,' xxiv. 543. The words of Achilles to Priam, a suppliant before him. Take that incomparable line and a half of Dante, Ugolino's tremendous words -

'Io no piangeva; si dentro impietrai.
Piangevan elli . . .'
take the lovely words of Beatrice to Virgil -
'Io son fatta da Dio, sua merce, tale,
Che la vostra miseria non mi tange,
Ne fiamma d' esto incendio non m'assale . . .'
take the simple, but perfect, single line -
"In la sua volontade e nostra pace."
Take of Shakespeare a line or two of Henry the Fourth's expostulation with sleep
"Wilt thou upon the high and giddy mast

Seal up the ship - boy's eyes, and rock his brains
"In cradle of the rude imperious surge"
and take, as well, Hamlet's dying request to Horatio -
"If thou didst ever hold me in thy heart,
Absent thee from felicity awhile,
And in this harsh world draw thy breath in pain
To tell my story . . ."
Take of Milton that Miltonic passage:
'Darken'd so, yet shone
Above them all the archangel; but his face
Deep scars of thunder had intrench'd, and care
Sat on his faded cheek . . .'
add two such lines as -
"And courage never to submit or yield
And what is else not to be overcome . . ."
and finish with the exquisite close to
the loss of Proserpine, the loss
" . . . which cost Ceres all that pain
To seek her through the world."

These few lines, if we have tact and can use them, are enough even of themselves to keep clear and sound our judgments about poetry, to save us from fallacious estimates of it, to conduct us to a real estimate.

The specimens I have quoted differ widely from one another, but they have in common this: the possession of the very highest poetical quality. If we are thoroughly penetrated by their power, we shall find that we have acquired a sense enabling us, whatever poetry may be laid before us, to feel the degree in which a high poetical quality is present or wanting there. Critics give themselves great labour to draw out what in the abstract constitutes the characters of a high quality of poetry. It is much better simply to have recourse to concrete examples; - to take specimens of poetry of the high, the very highest quality, and to say: The characters of a high quality of poetry are what is expressed there. They are far better recognised by being felt in the verse of the master, than by being perused in the prose of the critic. Nevertheless if we are urgently pressed to give some critical account of them, we may safely, perhaps, venture on laying down, not indeed how and why the characters arise, but where and in what they arise. They are in the matter and substance of the poetry, and they are in its manner and style. Both of these, the substance and matter on the one hand, the style and manner on the other, have a mark, an accent, of high beauty, worth, and power. But if we are asked to define this mark and accent in the abstract, our answer must be: No, for we should thereby be darkening the question, not clearing it. The mark and accent are as given by the substance and matter of that poetry, by the style and manner of that poetry, and of all other poetry which is akin to it in quality.

Only one thing we may add as to the substance and matter of poetry, guiding ourselves by Aristotle's profound observation that the superiority of poetry over history consists in its possessing a higher truth and a higher seriousness. Let us add, therefore, to what we have said, this: that the substances and matter of the best poetry acquire their special character from possessing, in an eminent degree, truth and seriousness. We may add yet further, what is in itself evident, that to the style and manner of the best poetry their special character, their accent, is given by their diction, and, even yet more, by their movement. And though we distinguish between the two characters, the two accents, of superiority, yet they are nevertheless vitally connected one with the other. The superior character of truth and seriousness, in the matter and substance of the best poetry, is inseparable from the superiority of diction and movement marking its style and manner. The two superiorities are closely related, and are in steadfast proportion one to the other. So far as high poetic truth and seriousness are wanting to a poet's matter and substance, so far also, we may be sure, will a high poetic stamp of diction and movement be wanting to his style and manner. In proportion as this high stamp of diction and movement, again, is absent from a poet's style and manner, we shall find, also, that high poetic truth and seriousness are absent from his substance and matter.

So stated, these are but dry generalities; their whole force lies in their application. And I could wish every student of poetry to make the application of them for himself. Made by himself, the application would impress itself upon his mind far more deeply than made by me. Neither will my limits allow me to make any full application of the generalities above propounded; but in the hope of bringing out, at any rate, some significance in them, and of establishing an important principle more firmly by their means, I will, in the space which remains to me, follow rapidly from the commencement the course of our English poetry with them in my view.

Once more I return to the early poetry of France, with which our own poetry, in its origins, is indissolubly connected. In the twelfth and thirteenth centuries, that seed time of all modern language and literature, the poetry of France had a clear predominance in Europe. Of the two divisions of that poetry, its productions in the langue d'oil and its productions in the langue d'oc, the poetry of the langue d'oc, of southern France, of the troubadours, is of importance because of its effect on Italian literature; - the first literature of modern Europe to strike the true and grand note, and to bring forth, as in Dante and Petrarch it brought forth, classics. But the predominance of French poetry in Europe, during the twelfth and thirteenth centuries, is due to its poetry of the langue d'oil, the poetry of northern France and of the tongue which is now the French language. In the twelfth century the bloom of this romance - poetry was earlier and stronger in England, at the court of our Anglo - Norman kings, than in France itself. But it was a bloom of French poetry; and as our native poetry formed itself, it formed itself out of this. The romance - poems which took possession of the heart and imagination of Europe in the twelfth and thirteenth centuries are French; they are,' as Southey justly says, 'the pride of French literature, nor have we anything which can be placed in competition with them. 'Themes were supplied from all quarters; but the romance - setting which was common to them all, and which gained the ear of Europe, was French. This constituted for the French poetry, literature, and language, at the height of the Middle Age, an unchallenged predominance. The Italian Brunetto Latini, the master of Dante, wrote his Treasure in French because, he says, 'la parleure en est plus delitable et plus commune a toutes gens.' In the same century, the thirteenth, the French romance - writer, Christian of Troyes, formulates the claims, in chivalry and letters, of France, his native country, as follows: -

'Or vous ert par cę livre apris,
Que Gresse ot de chevalerie
Le premier los et de clergie;
Puis vint chevalerie a Rome,

Et de la clergie la some,
Qui ore est en France venue.
Diex doinst qu'ele i soit retenue,
Et que li lius li abelisse
Tant que de France n'isse
L'onor qui s'i est arestee!'

"Now by this book you will learn that first Greece had the renown for chivalry and letters: then chivalry and the primacy in letters passed to Rome, and now it is come to France. God grant it may be kept there; and that the place may please it so well, that the honour which has come to make stay in France may never depart thence!" Yet it is now all gone, this French romance - poetry of which the weight of substance and the power of style are not unfairly represented by this extract from Christian of Troyes. Only by means of the historic estimate can we persuade ourselves not to think that any of it is of poetical importance.

But in the fourteenth century there comes an Englishman nourished on this poetry, taught his trade by this poetry, getting words, rhyme, metre from this poetry; for even of that stanza which the Italians used, and which Chaucer derived immediately from the Italians, the basis and suggestion was probably given in France. Chaucer (I have already named him) fascinated his contemporaries, but so too did Christian of Troyes and Wolfram of Eschenbach. Chaucer's power of fascination, however, is enduring; his poetical importance does not need the assistance of the historic estimate; it is real. He is a genuine source of joy and strength, which is flowing still for us and will flow always. He will be read, as time goes on, far more generally than he is read now. His language is a cause of difficulty for us; but so also, and I think in quite as great a degree, is the language of Burns. In Chaucer's case, as in that of Burns, it is a difficulty to be unhesitatingly accepted and overcome.

If we ask ourselves wherein consists the immense superiority of Chaucer's poetry over the romance - poetry - why it is that in passing from this to Chaucer we suddenly feel ourselves to be in another world, we shall find that his superiority is both in the substance of his poetry and in the style of his poetry. His superiority in substance is given by his large, free, simple, clear yet kindly view of human life, - so unlike the total want, in the romance - poets, of all intelligent command of it. Chaucer has not their helplessness; he has gained the power to survey the world from a central, a truly human point of view. We have only to call to mind the Prologue to The Canterbury Tales. The right comment upon it is Dryden's: 'It is sufficient to say, according to the proverb, that here is God's plenty.' And again: 'He is a perpetual fountain of good sense.' It is by a large, free, sound representation of things, that poetry, this high criticism of life, has truth of substance; and Chaucer's poetry has truth of substance.

Of his style and manner, if we think first of the romance - poetry and then of Chaucer's divine liquidness of diction, his divine fluidity of movement, it is difficult to speak temperately. They are irresistible, and justify all the rapture with which his successors speak of his 'gold dew - drops of speech.' Johnson misses the point entirely when he finds fault with Dryden for ascribing to Chaucer the first refinement of our numbers, and says that Gower also can show smooth numbers and easy rhymes. The refinement of our numbers means something far more than this. A nation may have versifiers with smooth numbers and easy rhymes, and yet may have no real poetry at all. Chaucer is the father of our splendid English poetry; he is our 'well of English undefiled,' because by the lovely charm of his diction, the lovely charm of his movement, he makes an epoch and founds a tradition. In Spenser, Shakespeare, Milton, Keats, we can follow the tradition of the liquid diction, the fluid movement of Chaucer; at one time it is his liquid diction of which in these poets we feel the virtue, and at another time it is his fluid movement. And the virtue is irresistible.

Bounded as is my space, I must yet find room for an example of Chaucer's virtue, as I have given examples to show the virtue of the great classics. I feel disposed to say that a single line is enough to show the charm of Chaucer's verse; that merely one line like this -

'O martyr souded in virginitee!' has a virtue of manner and movement such as we shall not find in all the verse of romance - poetry; - but this is saying nothing. The virtue is such as we shall not find, perhaps, in all English poetry, outside the poets whom I have named as the special inheritors of Chaucer's tradition. A single line, however, is too little if we have not the strain of Chaucer's verse well in our memory; let us take a stanza. It is from The Prioress 'Tale, the story of the Christian child murdered in a Jewry -

'My throte is cut unto my nekke - bone
Saide this child, and as by way of kinde
I should have deyd, yea, longe time agone;
But Jesu Christ, as ye in bookes finde,
Will that his glory last and be in minde,
And for the worship of his mother dere
Yet may I sing O Alma loud and clere.'

Wordsworth has modernised this Tale, and to feel how delicate and evanescent is the charm of verse, we have only to read Wordsworth's first three lines of this stanza after Chaucer's -

> *'My throat is cut unto the bone, I trow,*
> *Said this young child, and by the law of kind*
> *I should have died, yea, many hours ago.'*

The charm is departed. It is often said that the power of liquidness and fluidity in Chaucer's verse was dependent upon a free, a licentious dealing with language, such as is now impossible; upon a liberty, such as Burns too enjoyed, of making words like neck, bird, into a disyllable by adding to them, and words like cause, rhyme, into a disyllable by sounding the e mute. It is true that Chaucer's fluidity is conjoined with this liberty, and is admirably served by it; but we ought not to say that it was dependent upon it. It was dependent upon his talent. Other poets with a like liberty do not attain to the fluidity of Chaucer; Burns himself does not attain to it. Poets, again, who have a talent akin to Chaucer's, such as Shakespeare or Keats, have known how to attain his fluidity without the like liberty.

And yet Chaucer is not one of the great classics. His poetry transcends and effaces, easily and without effort, all the romance - poetry of Catholic Christendom; it transcends and effaces all the English poetry contemporary with it, it transcends and effaces all the English poetry subsequent to it down to the age of Elizabeth. Of such avail is poetic truth of substance, in its natural and necessary union with poetic truth of style. And yet, I say, Chaucer is not one of the great classics. He has not their accent. What is wanting to him is suggested by the mere mention of the name of the first great classic of Christendom, the immortal poet who died eighty years before Chaucer, - Dante. The accent of such verse as 'In la sua volontade e nostra pace' . . . is altogether beyond Chaucer's reach; we praise him, but we feel that this accent is out of the question for him. It may be said that it was necessarily out of the reach of any poet in the England of that stage of growth. Possibly; but we are to adopt a real, not a historic, estimate of poetry. However we may account for its absence, something is wanting, then, to the poetry of Chaucer, which poetry must have before it can be placed in the glorious class of the best. And there is no doubt what that something is. It is the bnoudalorns, the high and excellent seriousness, which Aristotle assigns as one of the grand virtues of poetry. The substance of Chaucer's poetry, his view of things and his criticism of life, has largeness, freedom, shrewdness, benignity; but it has not this high seriousness. Homer's criticism of life has it, Dante's has it, Shakespeare's has it. It is this chiefly which gives to our spirits what they can rest upon; and with the increasing demands of our modern ages upon poetry, this virtue of giving us what we can rest upon will be more and more highly esteemed. A voice from the slums of Paris, fifty or sixty years after Chaucer, the voice of poor Villon out of his life of riot and crime, has at its happy moments (as, for instance, in the last stanza of La Belle Heaulmiere∧7) more of this important poetic virtue of seriousness than all the productions of Chaucer. But its apparition in Villon, and in men like Villon, is fitful; the greatness of the great poets, the power of their criticism of life, is that their virtue is sustained.

'Ainsi le bon temps regretons
Entre nous, pauvres vieilles sottes,
Assises bas, a croppetons,
Tout en ung tas comme pelottes;
A petit feu de chenevottes
Tost allumees, tost estainctes.
Et jadis fusmes si mignottes!
Ainsi en prend a maintz et maintes.'

"Thus amongst ourselves we regret the good time, poor silly old things, low - seated on our heels, all in a heap like so many balls; by a little fire of hemp - stalks, soon lighted, soon spent. And once we were such darlings! So fares it with many and many a one."

To our praise, therefore, of Chaucer as a poet there must be this limitation; he lacks the high seriousness of the great classics, and therewith an important part of their virtue. Still, the main fact for us to bear in mind about Chaucer is his sterling value according to that real estimate which we firmly adopt for all poets. He has poetic truth of substance, though he has not high poetic seriousness, and corresponding to his truth of substance he has an exquisite virtue of style and manner. With him is born our real poetry.

For my present purpose I need not dwell on our Elizabethan poetry, or on the continuation and close of this poetry in Milton. We all of us profess to be agreed in the estimate of this poetry; we all of us recognise it as great poetry, our greatest, and Shakespeare and Milton as our poetical classics. The real estimate, here, has universal currency. With the next age of our poetry divergency and difficulty begin. An historic estimate of that poetry has established itself; and the question is, whether it will be found to coincide with the real estimate.

The age of Dryden, together with our whole eighteenth century which followed it, sincerely believed itself to have produced poetical classics of its own, and even to have made advance, in poetry, beyond all its predecessors. Dryden regards as not seriously disputable the opinion that the sweetness of English verse was never understood or practised by our fathers.' Cowley could see nothing at all in Chaucer's poetry. Dryden heartily admired it, and, as we have seen, praised its matter admirably; but of its exquisite manner and movement all he can find to say is that 'there is the rude sweetness of a Scotch tune in it, which is natural and pleasing, though not perfect.' Addison, wishing to praise Chaucer's numbers, compares them with Dryden's own. And all through the eighteenth century, and down even into our own times, the stereotyped phrase of approbation for good verse found in our early poetry has been, that it even approached the verse of Dryden, Addison, Pope, and Johnson.

Are Dryden and Pope poetical classics? Is the historic estimate, which represents them as such, and which has been so long established that it cannot easily give way, the real estimate? Wordsworth and Coleridge, as is well known, denied it; but the authority of Wordsworth and Coleridge does not weigh much with the young generation, and there are many signs to show that the eighteenth century and its judgments are coming into favour again. Are the favourite poets of the eighteenth century classics?

It is impossible within my present limits to discuss the question fully. And what man of letters would not shrink from seeming to dispose dictatorially of the claims of two men who are, at any rate, such masters in letters as Dryden and Pope; two men of such admirable talent, both of them, and one of them, Dryden, a man, on all sides, of such energetic and genial power? And yet, if we are to gain the full benefit from poetry, we must have the real estimate of it. I cast about for some mode of arriving, in the present case, at such an estimate without offence. And perhaps the best way is to begin, as it is easy to begin, with cordial praise.

When we find Chapman, the Elizabethan translator of Homer, expressing himself in this preface thus: "Though truth in her very nakedness sits in so deep a pit, that from Gades to Aurora and Ganges few eyes can sound her, I hope yet those few here will so discover and confirm that, the date being out of her darkness in this morning of our poet, he shall now gird his temples with the sun,' - we pronounce that such a prose is intolerable. When we find Milton writing: 'And long it was not after, when I was confirmed in this opinion, that he, who would not be frustrate of his hope to write well hereafter in laudable things, ought himself to be a true poem,' - we pronounce that such a prose has its own grandeur, but that it is obsolete and inconvenient. But when we find Dryden telling us: 'What Virgil wrote in the vigour of his age, in plenty and at ease, I have undertaken to translate in my declining years; struggling with wants, oppressed with sickness, curbed in my genius, liable to be misconstrued in all I write,' - then we exclaim that here at last we have the true English prose, a prose such as we would all gladly use if we only knew how. Yet Dryden was Milton's contemporary.

But after the Restoration the time had come when our nation felt the imperious need of a fit prose. So, too, the time had likewise come when our nation felt the imperious need of freeing itself from the absorbing preoccupation which religion in the Puritan age had exercised. It was impossible that this freedom should be brought about without some negative excess, without some neglect and impairment of the religious life of the soul; and the spiritual history of the eighteenth century shows us that the freedom was not achieved without them. Still, the freedom was achieved; the preoccupation, an undoubtedly baneful and retarding one if it had continued, was got rid of. And as with religion amongst us at that period, so it was also with letters. A fit prose was a necessity; but it was impossible that a fit prose should establish itself amongst us without some touch of frost to the imaginative life of the soul. The needful qualities for a fit prose are regularity, uniformity, precision, balance. The men of letters, whose destiny it may be to bring their nation to the attainment of a fit prose, must of necessity, whether they work in prose or in verse, give a predominating, an almost exclusive attention to the qualities of regularity, uniformity, precision, balance. But an almost exclusive attention to these qualities involves some repression and silencing of poetry.

We are to regard Dryden as the puissant and glorious founder, Pope as the splendid high priest, of our age of prose and reason, of our excellent and indispensable eighteenth century. For the purposes of their mission and destiny their poetry, like their prose, is admirable. Do you ask me whether Dryden's verse, take it almost where you will, is not good?

> '*A milk - white Hind, immortal and unchanged,*
> *Fed on the lawns and in the forest ranged.*'

I answer: Admirable for the purposes of the inaugurator of an age of prose and reason. Do you ask me whether Pope's verse, take it almost where you will, is not good?

'To Hounslow Heath I point, and Banstead Down;
'Thence comes your mutton, and these chicks my own.'

I answer: Admirable for the purposes of the high priest of an age of prose and reason. But do you ask me whether such verse proceeds from men with an adequate poetic criticism of life, from men whose criticism of life has a high seriousness, or even, without that high seriousness, has poetic largeness, freedom, insight, benignity? Do you ask me whether the application of ideas to life in the verse of these men, often a powerful application, no doubt, is a powerful poetic application? Do you ask me whether the poetry of these men has either the matter or the inseparable manner of such an adequate poetic criticism; whether it has the accent of

'Absent thee from felicity awhile ...'
or of
'And what is else not to be overcome ...'
or of
'O martyr souded in virginitee!'

I answer: It has not and cannot have them; it is the poetry of the builders of an age of prose and reason. Though they may write in verse, though they may in a certain sense be masters of the art of versification, Dryden and Pope are not classics of our poetry, they are classics of our prose.

Gray is our poetical classic of that literature and age; the position of Gray is singular, and demands a word of notice here. He has not the volume or the power of poets who, coming in times more favourable, have attained to an independent criticism of life. But he lived with the great poets, he lived, above all, with the Greeks, through perpetually studying and enjoying them; and he caught their poetic point of view for regarding life, caught their poetic manner. The point of view and the manner are not self - sprung in him, he caught them of others; and he had not the free and abundant use of them. But, whereas Addison and Pope never had the use of them, Gray had the use of them at times. He is the scantiest and frailest of classics in our poetry, but he is a classic.

And now, after Gray, we are met, as we draw towards the end of the eighteenth century, we are met by the great name of Burns. We enter now on times where the personal estimate of poets begins to be rife, and where the real estimate of them is not reached without difficulty. But in spite of the disturbing pressures of personal partiality, of national partiality, let us try to reach a real estimate of the poetry of Burns.

By his English poetry Burns in general belongs to the eighteenth century, and has little importance for us.

'Mark ruffian Violence, distain'd with crimes,
Rousing elate in these degenerate times;
View unsuspecting Innocence a prey,
As guileful Fraud points out the erring way;
While subtle Litigation's pliant tongue
The life - blood equal sucks of Right and Wrong!'

Evidently this is not the real Burns, or his name and fame would have disappeared long ago. Nor is Clarinda's love - poet, Sylvander, the real Burns either. But he tells us himself: 'These English songs gravel me to death. I have not the command of the language that I have of my native tongue. In fact, I think that my ideas are more barren in English than in Scotch. I have been at Duncan Gray to dress it in English, but all I can do is desperately stupid.' We English turn naturally, in Burns, to the poems in our own language, because we can read them easily; but in those poems we have not the real Burns.

The real Burns is of course in this Scotch poems. Let us boldly say that of much of this poetry, a poetry dealing perpetually with Scotch drink, Scotch religion, and Scotch manners, A Scotchman's estimate is apt to be personal. A Scotchman is used to this world of Scotch drink, Scotch religion, and Scotch manners; he has a tenderness for it; he meets its poet halfway. In this tender mood he reads pieces like the Holy Fair or Halloween. But this world of Scotch drink, Scotch religion, and Scotch manners is against a poet, not for him, when it is not a partial countryman who reads him; for in itself it is not a beautiful world, and no one can deny that it is of advantage to a poet to deal with a beautiful world. Burns' world of Scotch drink, Scotch religion, and Scotch manners, is often a harsh, a sordid, a repulsive world: even the world of his Cotter's Saturday Night is not a beautiful world. No doubt a poet's criticism of life may have such truth and power that it triumphs over its world and delights us. Burns may triumph over his world, often he does triumph over his world, but let us observe how and where. Burns is the first case we have had where the bias of the personal estimate tends to mislead; let us look at him closely, he can bear it.

Many of his admirers will tell us that we have Burns, convivial, genuine, delightful, here

'Leeze me on drink! it gies us mair
Than either school or college;
It kindles wit, it waukens lair,
It pangs us fou o'knowledge.
Be't whisky gill or penny wheep
Or only stronger potion,
It never fails, on drinking deep,

To kittle up our notion
By night or day.'

There is a great deal of that sort of thing in Burns, and it is unsatisfactory, not because it is bacchanalian poetry, but because it has not that accent of sincerity which bacchanalian poetry, to do it justice, very often has. There is something in it of bravado, something which makes us feel that we have not the man speaking to us with his real voice; something, therefore, poetically unsound.

With still more confidence will his admirers tell us that we have the genuine Burns, the great poet, when his strain asserts the independence, equality, dignity, of men, as in the famous song For a' that, and a 'that -

'A prince can mak' a belted knight,
A marquis, duke, and a' that;
But an honest man's aboon his might,
Guid faith he mauna fa' that!
For a' that, and a' that,
Their dignities, and a' that,
The pith o' sense, a pride o' worth,
Are higher rank than a' that.'

Here they find his grand, genuine touches; and still more, when this puissant genius, who so often set morality at defiance, falls moralising -

'The sacred lowe o' weel - placed love
Luxuriantly indulge it;
But never tempt th' illicit rove,
Tho' naething should divulge it.
I waive the quantum o' the sin,
The hazard o' concealing,
But och! it hardens a' within,
And petrifies the feeling.'

Or in a higher strain -
'Who made the heart, 'tis He alone
Decidedly can try us;
He knows each chord, its various tone;
Each spring, its various bias.
Then at the balance let's be mute,
We never can adjust it;

What's done we partly may compute, But know not what's resisted.'

Or in a better strain yet, a strain, his admirers will say, unsurpassable -

To make a happy fireside clime
To weans and wife,
That's the true pathos and sublime
Of human life.'

There is criticism of life for you, the admirers of Burns will say to us; there is the application of ideas to life! There is, undoubtedly. The doctrine of the last - quoted lines coincides almost exactly with what was the aim and end, Xenophon tells us, of all the teaching of Socrates. And the application is a powerful one; made by a man of vigorous understanding, and (need I say?) a master of language.

But for supreme poetical success more is required than the powerful application of ideas to life; it must be an application under the conditions fixed by the laws of poetic truth and poetic beauty. Those laws fix as an essential condition, in the poet's treatment of such matters as are here in question, high seriousness; - the high seriousness which comes from absolute sincerity. The accent of high seriousness, born of absolute sincerity, is what gives to such verse as -

'In la sua volontade e nostra pace . . .'

To such criticism of life as Dante's, its power. Is this accent felt in the passages which I have been quoting from Burns? Surely not; surely, if our sense is quick, we must perceive that we have not in those passages a voice from the very inmost soul of the genuine Burns; he is not speaking to us from these depths, he is more or less preaching. And the compensation for admiring such passages less, from missing the perfect poetic accent in them, will be that we shall admire more the poetry where that accent is found.

No; Burns, like Chaucer, comes short of the high seriousness of the great classics, and the virtue of matter and manner which goes with that high seriousness is wanting to his work. At moments he touches it in a profound and passionate melancholy, as in those four immortal lines taken by Byron as a motto for The Bride of Abydos, but which have in them a depth of poetic quality such as resides in no verse of Byro's own -

'Had we never loved sae kindly,
Had we never loved sae blindly,
Never met, or never parted,
We had ne'er been broken - hearted.'

But a whole poem of that quality Burns cannot make; the rest, in the *Farewell to Nancy,* is verbiage.

We arrive best at the real estimate of Burns, I think, by conceiving his work as having truth of matter and truth of manner, but not the accent or the poetic virtue of the highest masters. His genuine criticism of life, when the sheer poet in him speaks, is ironic; it is not -

'Thou Power Supreme, whose mighty scheme
These woes of mine fulfil,
Here firm I rest, they must be best
Because they are Thy will!'

It is far rather: *Whistle owre the lave o't*! Yet we may say of him as of Chaucer, that of life and the world, as they come before him, his view is large, free, shrewd, benignant, - truly poetic therefore; and his manner of rendering what he sees is to match. But we must note, at the same time, his great difference from Chaucer. The freedom of Chaucer is heightened, in Burns, by a fiery, reckless energy; the benignity of Chaucer deepens, in Burns, into an overwhelming sense of the pathos of things; - of the pathos of human nature, the pathos, also, of non - human nature. Instead of the fluidity of Chaucer's manner, the manner of Burns has spring, boundless swiftness. Burns is by far the greater force, though he has perhaps less charm. The world of Chaucer is fairer, richer, more significant than that of Burns; but when the largeness and freedom of Burns get full sweep, as in *Tam o' Shanter*, or still more in that puissant and splendid production, *The Jolly Beggars*, his world may be what it will, his poetic genius triumphs over it. In the world of *The Jolly Beggars* there is more than hideousness and squalor, there is bestiality; yet the piece is a superb poetic success. It has a breadth, truth, and power which make the famous scene in Auerbach's Cellar, of Goethe's Faust, seem artificial and tame beside it, and which are only matched by Shakespeare and Aristophanes.

Here, where his largeness and freedom serve him so admirably, and also in those poems and songs where to shrewdness he adds infinite archness and wit, and to benignity infinite pathos, where his manner is flawless, and a perfect poetic whole is the result, - in things like the address to the mouse whose home he had ruined, in things like *Duncan Gray, Tam Glen, Whistle and I'll come to you, my Lad, Auld Lang Syne* (this list might be made much longer), - here we have the genuine Burns, of whom the real estimate must be high indeed. Not a classic, nor with the excellent bnoudalorns of the great classics, nor with a verse rising to a criticism of life and a virtue like theirs; but a poet with thorough truth of substance and an answering truth of style, giving us a poetry sound to the core. We all of us have a leaning towards the pathetic, and may be inclined perhaps to prize Burns most for his touches of piercing, sometimes almost intolerable, pathos; for verse like -

'We twa hae paidl't i 'the burn
From mornin' 'sun till dine;
But seas between us braid hae roar'd
Sin auld lang syne . . .'

Where he is as lovely as he is sound. But perhaps it is by the perfection of soundness of his lighter and archer masterpieces that he is poetically most wholesome for us. For the votary misled by a personal estimate of Shelley, as so many of us have been, are, and will be, - of that beautiful spirit building his many - coloured haze of words and images

'Pinnacled dim in the intense inane' -

No contact can be wholesome than the contact with Burns at his archest and soundest. Side by side with the

'On the brink of the night and the morning
My coursers are wont to respire,
But the Earth has just whispered a warning
That their flight must be swifter than fire . . .'

of Prometheus Unbound, how salutary, how very salutary, to place this from Tam Glen -

'My minnie does constantly deave me
And bids me beware o' young men;

They flatter, she says, to deceive me;
But wha can think sae o' Tam Glen?'

But we enter on burning ground as we approach the poetry of times so near to us - poetry like that of Byron, Shelley, and Wordsworth - of which the estimates are so often not only personal, but personal with passion. For my purpose, it is enough to have taken the single case of Burns, the first poet we come to of whose work the estimate formed is evidently apt to be personal, and to have suggested how we may proceed, using the poetry of the great classics as a sort of touchstone, to correct this estimate, as we had previously corrected by the same means the historic estimate where we met with it. A collection like the present, with its succession of celebrated names and celebrated poems, offers a good opportunity to us for resolutely endeavouring to make our estimates of poetry real. I have sought to point out a method which will help us in making them so, and to exhibit it in use so far as to put any one who likes in a way of applying it for himself.

At any rate the end to which the method and the estimate are designed to lead, and from leading to which, if they do lead to it, they get their whole value, - the benefit of being able clearly to feel and deeply to enjoy the best, the truly classic, in poetry, - is an end, let me say it once more at parting, of supreme importance. We are often told that an era is opening in which we are to see multitudes of a common sort of readers, and masses of a common sort of literature; that such readers do not want and could not relish anything better than such literature, and that to provide it is becoming a vast and profitable industry. Even if good literature entirely lost currency with the world, it would still be abundantly worth while to continue to enjoy it by oneself. But it never will lose currency with the world, in spite of momentary appearances; it never will lose supremacy. Currency and supremacy are insured to it, not indeed by the world's deliberate and conscious choice, but by something far deeper, - by the instinct of self - preservation in humanity.

(b) NOTES AND EXPLANATIONS

"The future of poetry" etc. The opening paragraph is a quotation from the introduction Arnold had contributed to the volume dealing with poetry in a book called The Hundred Greatest Men (1879). T.S. Eliot has said that Arnold is here affirming that the emotions of Christianity can and must be preserved without the belief. Arnold is, however, essentially religious and moral; he believes, as does I.A. Richards, that in poetry the religious, moral and aesthetic sentiments coalesce. The result is different from philosophy on the one hand and science on the other; it is a special kind of knowledge which takes us straight to the object; it gives us knowledge by identity, its feeling and thought together. It is worth noting how Arnold makes a distinction between historical facts and ideas which become facts. Arnold's word 'idea' means the same thing as myth or symbol, a key concept in modern critical parlance.

Accredited dogma: A body of religious doctrines accepted as absolute truths.

Our religion divine illusion: Arnold, while: discussing the immense future of poetry, which will eventually take the place of religion, takes occasion to make a distinction between religious truth and poetic truth. Christianity, the religion of Europe, was based upon certain stories which were for centuries taken to be historical facts-such stories as the Fall of Man and his banishment; the immaculate birth of Christ, son of God; his crucifixion and resurrection etc. Christianity attached emotions to these facts, which were disproved by - 'her criticism' and religion, lost its very foundation. But poetry deals with ideas not with facts, and ideas belong to the world of human feeling; the primary affections of the human heart. Thus, poetry is not interested, for example, in the life of Christ, but in the ideas he stood for, such as love, self sacrifice, hate the sin but not the sinner. These ideas embodied, in the facts constitute the poetry of religion, and Arnold says that ideas are the soul of -poetry, for poetry is the grand .application of ideas to life. The 'other elements, beauty of language, of form, music and imagery though charming in their own way are not the substance of poetry, but its external glamour.

In the present work: Namely, - English Poets by T.H. Ward, to which this essay was an introduction. Ward's book was intended to trace the history of English poetry, which is only one stream in the: total volume of European poetry. Arnold insisted that for cultural purposes Europe was a single unit and English literature and culture formed only a part of it. He even agreed with Goethe that we should think of the world poetry as a mighty river of which the poetry of a nation was a small tributary.

For finely and truly does Wordsworth etc: Arnold asserts that as time rolls on mankind will come to depend more and more on the poetic interpretation of life for its consolation and spiritual strength. Without poetry philosophy will be empty and science incomplete. Then he quotes two sentences from a famous passage in Wordsworth's Preface to the Lyrical Ballads (1800).

In the first Wordsworth means to say that what animates science and makes it inspiring to the beholders is poetry. In the second fragment the same idea is applied to knowledge which remains cold and inert till it is impregnated with the spirit of poetry. Poetry makes it something living and breathing. The meaning is that abstract knowledge, scientific or philosophical is made vivid and lively for the people by poetry.

Sainte Beuve: (1804-18 69) the great French critic, whom Arnold regarded as an ideal critic.

Charlatanism: Pretence, imposture, fraud.

In poetry as criticism of life etc.: Arnold famous and controversial definition of poetry falls into two parts: (i) **Poetry is the criticism of life:** (ii) But this criticism must be governed by the laws of poetic beauty and poetic truth. By criticism' Arnold means interpretation: Poetry is the interpretation of life, natural and moral, which heightens our interest in and deepens our understanding of human life and human nature. But this criticism should have poetic beauty which arises from the largeness of the view point and the beauty of form and expression in the communication of this view to the readers. The second law is poetic truth which is different from the truth of philosophy or of science.

The poet is not interested in abstract truths and he is not a dealer in mere precepts. His truth is 'concrete and sensuous; it is embodied in a story, dramatic or narrative which is interesting in itself and charges the truth with passion and emotion, so that it is 'carried alive into the heart of the reader', as Wordsworth puts it.

Pellisson: A seventeenth century French writer, author of 'A History of the French Academy'.

Politesse sterile et rampante: Politeness sterile and creeping. We may recall here Dryden's description of the 17th-century French classical drama; 'It is like a marble statue beautiful, but without blood.'

Charles d' Hericault: Pen name of the French novelist Charles Joseph de Ricault (1823-1899).

Clement Marot: (1496--1544) a French poet.

In poetry, as a criticism of life, etc.: Arnold later defines this phrase as an application of moral ideas to life; the poet telling us 'how to live.' The phrase may, therefore, mean an attempt to re-present life so as to transform life. This preoccupation with life and its transformation has its limitations as may be seen in Arnold's essay on Wordsworth which hardly speaks about the mystical-spiritual quality of Wordsworth's poetry. See also Arnold's essay on Shelley where Shelley is described as an 'ineffectual angel.' Neither the idealism of Shelley nor the realism of Burns or Chaucer could come under his, definition.

This kind of repeating of some key phrases and sentences, it may be noted, is one of the significant and often purposeful features of Arnold's prose style.

T. S. Eliot ridicules this favourite definition of Arnold's in his *The Use of Poetry and the Use of Criticism* (p. 111):

At bottom': that is a great way down; the bottom is the bottom. At the bottom of the abyss is what few ever see, and what those cannot bear to look at for long; and it is not a 'criticism of life.' If we mean life as a whole-not that Arnold ever saw life as a whole -from top to bottom can anything that we can say of it ultimately, of that awful mystery, be called criticism? We bring very little from our rare descents, and that is not criticism.

But the fundamental truth of Arnold's belief can survive Eliot's rhetoric of contempt. Eliot dismisses Arnold's experience of life as something shallow and negative for he holds that Arnold has seen something of the boredom but not the horror of life, not to speak of its glory. Eliot has obviously misunderstood the term 'criticism of life' which Arnold has used in the sense of presenting and at the same time evaluating life according to the best that has been thought and said.

The grand power of poetry is its interpretative power; by which I mean not a power of drawing out in black and white an explanation of the mystery of the universe verse, but the power of so dealing with things as to awaken in us a wonderfully full, new, and intimate sense of them, and of our relations with them. When this sense is awakened in us, as to objects without us, we feel ourselves to be in contact with the essential nature of those objects, to be no longer bewildered and oppressed by them, and this feeling calms and satisfies us as no other can. Poetry, indeed, interprets in another way besides this; but one of its two ways of interpreting, of exercising its highest power, is by awakening this sense in us. I will not now inquire whether this sense is illusive, whether it can be proved not to be illusive, whether it does absolutely make us possess the real nature of things; all I say is, that poetry can awaken it in us, and that to awaken it is one of the highest powers of poetry. The interpretations of science do not give us this intimate sense of objects as the interpretations of poetry give it; they appeal to a limited faculty, and not to the whole man.)

And these two functions are fused in Arnold's definition. For Eliot each art can present only one thing and no one discipline can take the place of another.

Arnold's view is an integrated view where the problem of how to live is confronted at all levels and resolved by poetry at its best.

The cloud of glory playing round a classic etc: The meaning is that it is difficult to form a true estimate of an old writer, because his very antiquity makes him an object of reverence and clothes him with a cloud of glory, so that the real man remains hidden behind his halo. He ceases to be a human being and becomes a God, like Jupiter, lord of all Greek gods who was seated in glory above the gods on mount Olympus.

Classic character: Arnold takes the word 'classic' in its original sense: 'belonging to the class or highest rank'.

Literary dilettantism: A superficial, non-serious attitude towards literature.

Methuselah A man who, according to the Bible, lived for 969 years.

True if time were not so short etc: Arnold is referring to the teaching of the classical languages, Greek and Latin, at English schools. The knowledge of the classics is useful and salutary beyond doubt, but much of the time is taken up with the historical analysis of the language. It is forgotten that time is short and the wit of the boys is limited in its capacity. An elaborate analysis of words may exhaust him and leave him without interest in and knowledge of the individual authors. The secret of true enjoyment is the emphasis on the essentials.

Imitation: a religious work by Thomas a Kempis (1380-1471) in Latin.

Cum multa etc 'When thou shalt have read and known many things, it will behove thee always to return to the one beginning. I am He who teacheth men knowledge'. (From 'Against Vain and Worldly Learning'.

Dangerous abuse of language: Because the language is used to praise a writer falsely, because he happens to be an old writer belonging to our national past. For example Caedmon, an Anglo-Saxon religious poet of seventh century has been compared to Milton. This is a gross exaggeration.

Joculater, Jongleur: Bards or comedians.

One thinks of Homer etc: Arnold has been illustrating the dangers inherent in the historic estimate of an author, who is praised beyond due proportion, which means a gross misuse of language. He cites the case of the ancient to French poem Chason de Roland, which is a document of the past and is interesting as a specimen of the Mediaeval French. But M. Vitet, a French critic, describes it as a grand monument of epic genius, grand in general conception and in details a combination of simplicity with greatness, which marks the epic of highest excellence. Arnold says that this high praise may be appropriate to Homer, the father of Greek epic rather than to an obscure French poet of the Middle Ages.

Now turn to Homer: Arnold quotes from Homer's Iliad. Helen is speaking of her two brothers so said she: They long since in Earth's soft-arms were reposing, these in their own dear land, their fatherland, Lacedaemon.

Address of Zeus etc: In the same Homeric epic: the address is, 'Ah' unhappy pair, why gave you we to king Peleus, to a mortal, but ye are without old age and immortal.

Achilles to Priam: Priam, the old king of Troy, went to the camp of the Greek warrior, Achilles, to beg him to hand over the dead body of Hector, his most glorious son, to him for decent burial. Proud Achilles said to him, 'we hear, thou, old man, in former days, wast happy.

Dante's Ugolino: Dante, the greatest Italian poet of the Middle Ages, composed his grand Christian poem, Divine Comedy, which has three divisions - Inferno (Hell); Purgatorio (Purgatory); Paradiso (Paradise). Dante meets the shade of Count Ugolino, who relates to him how he and his young children were locked to starve and die in tower.

Beatrice to Virgil: From Dante. Through Hell and Purgatory the guide of Dante is Virgil, the national poet of Rome, author of Aeneid but beyond that his guide is the blessed soul of Beatrice, his lady love on the earth.

Darkened so: Milton's description of Satan, the rebel, Archangel, who was defeated and hurled by God into Hell, along with his followers. Paradise Lost. Bkl.

Which cost Ceres: The reference is to the Greek story of goddess Ceres, whose daughter Proserpina was abducted by Pluto, King of the dark region of death: she wandered mournfully in search of her daughter and finally compelled to gods to grant that Proserpina should live for half the year with her mother.

Langue d' oil: The French language current in the region North of Loire, the other was the language Southern France.

Poetry of the troubadours: The great poetry of courtly love.

Petrarch: The celebrated Italian poet, next only to Dante, whose love-sonnets on Lady Laura were extremely influential in France and England.

Brunetto Latini: (1210-94) Italian philosopher and politician, author of Treasures, an encyclopedia in French, the language is most delightful and most commonly known among all peoples.

La parliem etc: Its language is universally more pleasing and moral.

That stanza: Known as the Rhyme Royal, a stanza of seven lines.
Wolfram Eschenbach: A German poet of the twelfth century.
Central and human point: Interest in man as man, in all his glory and his meanness.
Liquidness of diction and divine fluidity etc: Chaucer's style is smooth and soft by virtue of predominance of (liquid) consonants, l, M, n, r; and the movement of his lines is musical and flowing, one line seems to melt into another.
Gower: was a contemporary of Chaucer.
O martyr etc.: This is how the Prioress in her tale addresses the Christian boy murdered by the Jews. It is from Chaucer's masterpiece, The Canterbury Tales.
Villon: A French poet of 15th century who led a life of poverty and licentiousness and wove his experiences into his poetry, striking occasionally moving strains from his libertine's lyre. In the stanza of the poem alluded to in the remark a poor old prostitute is recalling, with deep nostalgia, her days of youth and much-prized beauty, yet to say that this single stanza is worth all the poetry of Chaucer is to fly in the face of public opinion and all canons of just criticism.
Restoration: Or the age of Dryden (1660-1700) so called because monarchy was restored in 1660 when King Charles II returned from France to rule as a sovereign of his people.
Imperious need of fit prose: Restoration marks the beginning of rationalism and it also saw the establishment of the Royal Society. These two were the symptoms of the era of prose.

Religion in the Puritan age: The Commonwealth period when Cromwell was the Lord President of England and the Puritans were so powerful that they closed all the theatres and banned public performances. The Restoration was a reaction against it, a surrender to carnal pleasures.

Some touch of frost: Cultivation of prose stresses reason and intellect; curbs the freedom of imagination and distrusts the divine frenzy. It freezes the soul.

Age of Prose and reason etc: In one sentence Arnold gives the essence of eighteenth century literature. It is an age of prose in poetry also which has the qualities of good prose, order, regularity, precision, restraint and balance, yet the century is excellent and indispensable because it developed the modern prose and the modern essay and popularised the new prose form, the novel, which has now become the epic of democracy and faithful mirror of modern consciousness.

Dryden and Pope Classics of Prose: Arnold has elaborated this statement by saying that poetry is conceived and composed in the soul, but the poetry of Dryden and Pope is conceived and composed in their wit.

Gray is one poetical classic: It is an exaggerated estimate, born of personal preference. Gray had many qualities in common with Arnold, such as love of Greek, melancholy nature, slight poetic output and sense of living in an uncongenial age.

The point of view etc.: Arnold implies that his philosophy and style were deeply coloured by his reading and both were kept under restraint.

Burns: Robert Burns the eighteenth century Scottish poet who was the son of a peasant and led a life of the poor plough man, with his love of wine and women and kinship with beggars and vagabonds. Yet he became suddenly popular and was carried to the company of noblemen and ladies on the crest of celebrity, which, alas! landed him again into the slough of poverty. Yet his gift of song was irrepressible and his springs of wit, human and love inexhaustible.

Mark ruffian violence: The passage shows some marks of the eighteenth century poetic diction; its preference for the music of the heroic couplet and for personification of abstract qualities.

Clarinda's love poet: Robert Burns corresponded with Mrs. M' Lehose (Clarinda) under a pen-name, Sylvander.

Cotton's Saturday Night: One of the best-known poems by Robert Burns. It gives a moving picture of the peasant's domestic life, its simplicity, family affection and sincere Piety.

Bacchanalian poetry. Poetry of wine: Bacchus is the Greek wine god.

The sacred love etc: Taken from Burns, 'Epistle to a Young Friend'.

To make a happy fire-side clime: From 'Epistle to Dr. Black-lock'.

Xenophon: A great Athenian of 5th century B.C., a disciple of the great teacher, Socrates. He has explained and defended the doctrines of Socrates in his Memorabilia. The essence of this wisdom which Arnold underlines here may be put in the words of Wordsworth:

Type of the wise that soar but never roam,
True to the kindred points of heaven and home.

In law Sua etc: From Dante : 'In His Will is Our Peace'.

'Goethe's Faust: The famous dramatic poem in two parts by the German poet and statesman Goethe. The subject is based on the legend already handled by Marlowe in his Dr. Faustus.

Aristophanes: (433-380 B.C.) Father of the old Greek comedy which blends lyricism, fantasy, mirth and ribaldry.

For the votary misled by Shelley: Arnold means to say that the sound, concrete and earth-bound poetry of Robert Burns is a healthy cure for the admirers of Shelley's poetry who with the music and colour of his words builds his airy kingdom in the bosom of the sky, remote from our spheres of joys and sorrows. In his essay on Shelley, Arnold pictures the poet as 'a beautiful and ineffectual angel beating in the void his luminous wings in vain', Arnold is criticising the ethereal luminous and insubstantial quality of Shelley's poetry. The quotation is taken from Shelley's lyrical drama, Prometheus Unbound. **By instinct of** *self preservation:* Arnold means to say that humanity will instinctively cling to great literature for preventing itself from spiritual and moral torpor.

(c) SUBSTANCE

(i) The essay begins with one of Arnold's own remarks concerning the immense future of poetry as the mainstay of mankind for consolation and solace. As the old religious tradition declines under the pressure of growing materialism its function of sustaining the hope of man will be taken over by poetry.

(ii) We must always keep in mind this high destiny of poetry and its indispensability for the perfection of man. Without poetry our science will remain incomplete, for Wordsworth has rightly observed that poetry is "the impassioned expression which is in the countenance of all sciences; it is the breath and finer spirit of all knowledge'.

(iii) Consistently with the dignity and the noble future role of science our standard of poetry should be high and we should be satisfied with nothing sort of the very best in poetry. Poetry of high order may be defined 'as a criticism of life under the conditions fixed for such a criticism by the laws of the poetic truth and poetic beauty. The criticism of life conveyed by best poetry will have the power of forming, sustaining and delighting us as nothing else does.

(iv) But in our endeavour to discover the best poetry we must guard against two dangers–the historic estimate and the personal estimate. The danger of the historic estimate lies in our tendency to over-estimate an author, conspicuous in his own age, but now obscure and forgotten. Likewise, the danger of the personal estimate becomes serious when we are estimating the worth of writers near to us in time and capable of arousing our preferences and prejudices in an atmosphere of confusion and vagueness about their genuine worth

The aim of a student of poetry should be to discover a classic, a poet of the first rank, who must be carefully read and frankly criticised for his occasional lapse and if, for all skepticism, he continues to give us enjoyment he is indeed a true classic.

(v) Our knowledge of such classics will help us in finding out the real quality of a modern work. We should have always in our minds lines and expressions of the great masters, Homer, Dante, Shakespeare and Milton, to serve as touchstones for detecting the presence or absence of the high poetic quality in the works under our examination. This way of judging the quality of great poetry by concrete examples is much more effective than the abstract statement about the nature of poetic excellence. Nevertheless if we are pressed to define this poetic excellence we may say that both the substance and matter on the one hand, and the style and manner on the other have a mark, an accent of high beauty, worth and power.

(vi) To this we may add one more quality, truth and seriousness. The two excellences are closely related so that of truth and high seriousness are lacking in a poem it will want high poetic stamp in matter and manner, and conversely in proportion as this high stamp on diction and movement is wanting there will be an absence of high poetic truth in the same degree.

(vii) We may now trace, in. brief terms, the history of English poetry which in its origins was closely connected with the French poetry. In twelfth and thirteenth centuries that seed time of all modern language and literature, the place of honour in Europe was occupied by the Poetry of France. Of this poetry, the division known as the poetry of the South, the poetry of the troubadours is significant because of its influence on the poetry of Italy-the first literature in Europe to strike the grand note and to produce, in Dante and Petrarch, the two first classics of European literature in the Middle Ages.

But it was the language of the North of France which exerted the deepest influence on the poetry of England in twelfth and thirteenth centuries. France produced a crop of romances which captured the heart and imagination of Europe and created a vogue in setting and symbolism. If the French poetry of the South kindled the poetic fire in Italy, the French poetry of the North impregnated the poetic soil in England and nursed the Muse of Chaucer, the morning star of English poetry. Chaucer, being a real genius, ultimately soared above their height and came within an ace of the grand position of a classic. While the French romances have now become the curiosities of the past, the stream of joy and strength rising from him is still flowing and will continue to flow. The difficulty of his language is there but it has to be overcome, as a similar hurdle in the case of Burns.

Chaucer's superiority over the French romances both in his substance and in style: The substance of his poetry is constituted by his large, free, simple, clear yet kindly view of human life, so manifest in his Prologue to the Canterbury Tales, his masterpiece. Dryden made the right comment upon the Prologue 'Here is God's Plenty', and upon its author, 'He is a perpetual foundation of good sense'. His poetry is the criticism of life; it has truth of substance. As regards his style it has long been praised for its divine liquidness of diction and divine fluidity of movement. His successors went into raptures over this 'gold dewdrops of speech'. Chaucer is the father of English poetry, 'the well of English undefiled', who originated a tradition in style, which embraces Spenser, Shakespeare, Milton and Keats.

But with all his superiority over his predecessor, in France and his successors in England, before Spenser, Chaucer is not one of the great classics. What he wants is 'the high and excellent seriousness which Aristotle assigns as one of the grand virtues of poetry'. Indeed, there is more seriousness in the last stanza of *La Belle Heaulmiere* composed by Villon in the slums of Paris than in all the poems of Chaucer, yet Chaucer's excellence in substance and style is very high and his greatness is independent of his historical prestige as the originator of real poetry in England.

It is not necessary to linger over Elizabethan poetry which begins with Spenser and ends with Milton. Its greatness and excellence are unquestioned and so is the position of Shakespeare and Milton, as the English poetical classics. But the poetry of the neo-classical period (1660-1800) which embraces Dryden at one end and Pope at the other is of doubtful prestige and deserves a closer scrutiny.

Both these poets have been over-praised for the refinement and polish of their numbers and time has now come to review their position in its historical context. After the Restoration (1660) time was ripe for the creation of fit prose. The nation had freed itself from the fetters of religious pre-occupation, but the freedom thus gained was productive, in its effect, of some impairment of the power of the soul. The result in literature was obvious; prose established itself but 'not without some touch of frost to the imaginative life of the soul'. The writers cultivated the needful qualities of prose, 'regularity; uniformity, precision and balance', which necessarily involved 'some repression and silencing of poetry'. Arnold, therefore, concludes, 'we are to regard Dryden as the puissant and glorious founder, and Pope as the splendid high priest, of our age of prose and reason, of our excellent and indispensable eighteenth century'. Their criticism of life lacks high seriousness and their grand application of ideas to life is not a powerful poetic application.

The poetical classic of that age of Pope is Thomas Gray. He lacks, of course, the volume and power of the great poets of more favourable ages, but he was steeped in the poetry of Greek masters and caught something of their view of life and their poetic manner. So he is one of the frailest of the classics but 'he is a classic'.

From Gray we pass to Burns, the Scottish poet who brings us to the brink of the time when personal estimate of a writer has scope for its play. Burns wrote in English as well as in Scottish dialect. His English poetry is an adaptation of the artificial 18th century poetic diction, and he himself has confessed, "But these English songs gravel me to death. I have not the command of language that I have over my native tongue'. The real Burns is, thus, in his Scotch poems, bulk of which deals with Scotch drink, Scotch religion' and Scotch manners. If is not a beautiful world, which is certainly of advantage to a poet. His world is often 'harsh, sordid and repulsive', but he often triumphs over it. This triumph has produced a body of poetry rich and various and his admirers have singled out the one or the other of its several facets some have praised him for his convivial songs, where he is frankly and delightfully hedonistic. More important still are the poems where he asserts the native independence, equality and dignity of men. For some the genuine Burns is found in those rare poems where he strikes a note of morality. Again, there are poems about domestic love and felicity where one is apt to discover 'criticism of life as well as grand application of ideas to life. But for supreme poetical success something more is required which his poems do not possess. Indeed, Burns, like Chaucer, falls short of high seriousness which rings in the-accents of Dante. Only in some single passages he strikes the note of profound and passionate melancholy, but he cannot sustain the note through a whole poem. His view of life, like that of Chaucer, is large, free, shrewd and benignant and the manner of rendering it 'is to match'. Indeed, the freedom of Chaucer is heightened in Burns by a fiery, reckless energy; and his benignity is deepened into a profound pathos of human life. Instead of Chaucer's fluidity of style his manner has buoyancy and leaping swiftness; he has less of charm but greater force. It is this force and energy which transmutes the bestiality of his world as in his 'The Jolly Beggars'. He is still greater in those songs where to his excellence he adds shrewdness archness and wit and produces whole pieces of uniform merit. He is a master of true pathos but his real greatness lies in his lighter, witty pieces, which place us amid creatures of flesh and blood. The poetry of Burns, therefore, will prove a salutary antidote to those who are deluded by the splendid but airy visions of Shelley.

It is not necessary to proceed further with this review of English poets. Suffice it to wind up the discussion with a passing glance at the complaint that in view of the lack of taste in the multitude of readers there is no future for great poetry. But, the author is confident that great poetry will never lose its currency, despite its temporary set back. This currency is insured not by the world's deliberate choice but by the natural instinct of self-preservation in humanity. Death of good poetry will involve the death of the human heart and soul.

(d) CRITICAL REMARKS

The Study of Poetry, which was brought out in 1880, as an introduction to The English Poets, by T. H. Ward–an anthology of English poetry in four volumes, is one of the best-known and most significant of Arnold's critical pieces. In this single essay the reader will find, in a nutshell, all that Arnold has to say about the future of poetry; about his own idea of highest poetry; about the best way of testing the genuineness' of a poem under examination, and the standard he applies to the individual poets for determining their intrinsic quality and their place in the history of Poetry. The essay contains most of his definitions and catch phrases about poetry which have become a part of the general stock of critical Phraseology.

(i) He is almost dogmatic and over-assertive about the immense future of poetry which is destined to become more and more consolation and stay for mankind as religion and philosophy gradually lose their force and cease to be effective. It is true that the growing multitude of half-educated readers will prefer cheap literature and high poetry will be relegated into the narrow circles of scholars and specialists. But Arnold is confident about the final recovery of poetry which mankind, guided by the instinct of self-preservation, will not suffer to sink into permanent oblivion.

(ii) The sum of what Arnold conceived as the distinguishing marks of poetry is present in this essay. Poetry is the criticism of life, but this criticism should be poetic and must be invested with the beauty and truth peculiar to poetry. Poetry is the grand application of ideas to life, and its most crucial note is high seriousness, in the absence of which all the excellence of matter and style in poetry fails to place a poet among the classics. Arnold has repeated these characteristics again and again as if he were anxious to hammer the points home to his readers.

Repetition, however, does not serve to enlighten the readers about Arnold's real meaning, because he has not cared to explain his phrases clearly.

(iii) The essay also contains Arnold's 'touch stone' method in criticism, which remains one of the most controversial points in Arnold criticism. Arnold says that the critic of poetry should have significant lines and fragments of the great poets in mind and absorb their spirit, so that he may carry in his heart a readymade touchstone for testing the genuine quality of a poem he has to judge. Critics have rightly pointed out that the method is arbitrary and may create chaos in the domain of poetic criticism.

(iv) In the next place, the essay affords fine illustrations of Arnold's power of bringing out the essence of a poet in a, few significant and memorable words. The reader has simply to glance at the paragraphs on Chaucer and Burns to be convinced of the truth of this statement. Equally significant is the brief but illuminating comparison between the two poets. The passage dealing with the 18th century, the age of prose and reason, is equally significant though many modern students will not agree with Arnold's estimate of Dryden and Pope as classics of prose rather of poetry. But Arnold simply means to say that Dryden and Pope lack that high imagination and grandeur of style which mark the great classics in poetry.

(v) That Arnold had his own limitations as a critic is also illustrated by this essay. He applies one uniform standard to all poets for judging their excellence. He places Dante and Chaucer in the same category and concludes that Chaucer lacks that high seriousness which is indispensable for a classic in poetry. His limitation becomes all the more serious and glaring when, guided by his partiality he places Gray not only about Dryden and Pope, but also above Chaucer and Burns, when he calls him a frail classic, but a classic indeed of poetry.

(vi) The essay abounds in quotations and reference to poets, English and continental, and clearly shows Arnold's scholarship, especially his partiality for the French poetry. It breathes the genuine love of poetry and the high, fastidious standard which Arnold applied to it. There are also significant statements in the essay memorable in their own way, and significant also for the counter-opinions that they have provoked. One such statement is the remark that it is of advantage for a poet to live in a beautiful world. Eliot has replied to Arnold that to live in a beautiful world is not so important for a poet. It is more important for him to be able to perceive the beauty beneath the glory and the boredom present in the world in which he has to live and to work. On the whole, the essay is extremely thought-provoking and stimulates the reader at every step to pause and think for himself in order to enjoy the full flavour of the author's fervent love and regard for poetry.

(e) SYMPOSIUM OF CRITICISM: A BRIEF CRITIQUE ON ARNOLD'S IDEA OF POETRY

Arnold was convinced that the future of poetry was immense, because with the decline of the orthodox religion, mankind will turn, more and more, to poetry for joy, consolation and elevation of mind. In view of this conviction Arnold was at pains to repeat the qualities which poetry must possess in order to be able to discharge its high function. And the poets whose performances, were marked by these characteristics were to be placed among the classics of poetry; that is, poets of the first rank like Homer, Dante, Shakespeare and Milton, whose style may conveniently be used as a touch-stone for testing the real worth of new poems.

The qualities of great poetry are defined by Arnold in a few memorable sentences, which unfortunately are not free from ambiguity and vagueness, and have to be examined very carefully.

Poetry as a criticism of life.

Arnold's first requirement of poetry of high excellence is that it should be 'a criticism of life under conditions fixed for such a criticism by the laws of the poetic truth and poetic beauty'. The term criticism should be taken, in the general sense, as interpretation of life, which Arnold uses elsewhere. The poetic interpretation may be two-fold: natural interpretation and moral interpretation of things external to man; and the interpretation of qualities within him, by virtue of which he is great or small, noble or ignoble. It is relevant to quote here one of Arnold's own observations:

"The grand power of poetry is its interpretative power by which I mean, not a power of drawing out any black and white explanation of the mystery of the universe, but the power of so dealing with things as to awaken in us wonderfully full, new, and intimate sense of them, and of our relations with them. When this sense is awakened in us, as to objects without us, we feel ourselves to be in contact with the essential nature of those objects, to be no longer bewildered and oppressed by them, but to have their secret and to be in harmony with them, and this feeling calms and satisfies us as no other feeling can."

This is the revealing power of poetry, the power of removing 'the films of familiarity' from the faces of things and revealing their beauty, dignity and mystery. Poetry teaches us the true way of knowing thing, knowing through love, sympathy and disinterestedness. This knowing is different from the knowing of science. In science knowledge is power: We know things in order to exploit them as things created for our use - we murder to dissect'.

Similar is the case with the moral interpretation which shows us the natural worth and status of men around us and links us with them by arousing our love, sympathy and fellow feeling. They cease to be factory hands to be exploited for our profit or creatures inferior to us because of their poverty or humble rank in society. They become our equals with the same organs, the same feeling heart, the same capacity for joy and sorrow. This is the meaning of the passionate protest of Shylock against the inhumanities of the Christians in regard to the Jews, in Shakespeare's Merchant of Venice: Hath not a Jew eyes? Hath not a Jew ears? If you tickle us will we not laugh? If you prick us will we not bleed? In one of his poems Wordsworth addresses a hasty human walker in feeling terms, 'Turn, turn thy hasty foot aside, do not tread on the poor worm!' why? because the body which you are going to destroy required a God to make.

Now this is also one of the grandest functions of religion, the difference lies in the ways of teaching. The religious teacher preaches by precepts and reminds us of our duties in abstract terms, but the poetic interpretation is bound by the laws of the poetic beauty and poetic truth. It is concrete, vivid and endowed with the beauty of form and phasing and the truth it conveys is poetic: it is steeped in feeling and invested with life and animation: it is winged with passion and flies direct to the heart of the audience and fills it to the brim with warmth.

Grand application of ideas to life.

The second characteristic of great poetry, according to Arnold, is grand application of ideas to life, to the problem, how to live! The manner of our living will depend on our conception of ourselves and also of other human beings and human life in general. If we believe ourselves to be the selfish, brutish and wicked creatures, living among a crowd of similar creatures, then we shall lead a life of fear, caution and fierce struggle and will convert the world into a darkling plain, where ignorant armies clash by night. Machiavelli conceived human beings as naturally base and wicked who can be tamed by force only, so he advised the kings and rulers of men to cultivate certain animal qualities-the strength of the lion and the cunning of the fox. The successful king must be a compound of the lion and the fox.

Similarly, philosophers and religionists who believed the world to be a vanity and living only a process of dying, or the flesh as a hindrance to the progress of the soul, thought it fit to retreat into the solitude, away from worldly temptations, in order to mortify the flesh to nourish the soul and prepare it for its entry into the eternal realms of light and permanent realities.

But majority of men have to live in the world and face the problems of life and in order that they live well they should be taught to entertain noble ideas about life, about themselves and about men and women around them. Addressing the capitalists of the Victorian age Ruskin stated that the sucking of the blood of human beings may be the practice worthy of the mosquito, but it can never become a human being made after the image of God.

Arnold means to say that great poetry, with the help of its verbal magic and passion-winged truth must fill the readers with noble ideas about human life, human nature and human duties so that they may learn to live nobly and contribute their own share to the beauty, dignity and nobility of human life. We may recall here the noble words of Wordsworth regarding the aim of his poetry: 'They will co-operate with the benign tendencies in human nature and society, and will, in their degree, be efficacious in making men wiser, better and happier.'

High seriousness

The third great quality of great poetry is high seriousness which informs its matter and manner. Arnold takes the word 'seriousness' from Aristotle's remark that poetry is more serious and philosophical than history because history deals with the particulars and poetry with the universal in the particular. So one meaning of 'seriousness' is universality. Poetry must deal with the depth of things and appeal to those primary affections of the human heart which are common to all human beings in all ages and climes and which remain intact below the changes constantly taking place on the surface. Seriousness, he further says, goes with sincerity; it is not only the revelation of the depth of things, but also an interpretation springing from the depth of the poet's own heart. He must have felt the deep mystery in the depth of his own heart so that his accents are the echoes of his own deep feelings.

But Arnold also means by 'seriousness' a tragic view of life and is obviously in agreement with W. B. Yeats, one of this great modern poets, that we begin to live indeed when we come to view life as a tragedy; because comedy deals with the surface of life, but tragedy with its depth. On this account Arnold does not regard Chaucer as a true classic. With all his poetic criticism of life and magic of language and diction Chaucer lacks high seriousness. In this connection he goes to the extent of saying that a single stanza in a poem on the prostitutes composed by Villon in the slums of Paris is worth all the productions of Chaucer. In the stanza under reference old prostitutes are reflecting sadly upon their' youthful days when the beauty and freshness of their prime made them real prizes in the eyes of their numerous admirers. The author of 'The Canterbury Tales' is essentially a comedian, watching with a smile the motley panorama of the Canterbury pilgrims as it unrolls itself before his interested gaze. This view of Chaucer will not be acceptable to most of his admirers, because his comedy is by no means superficial. It presents a faithful picture of a body of social representation caught in a holiday mood. They are a mixture of good and evil as other human beings are and Chaucer's comedy is as effective in revealing the badness of a character, as his or her goodness. Chaucer does not denounce evil in severe terms, but makes it a part of his survey as a necessary element of human life and human nature.

Apart from this apparent injustice to Chaucer, Arnold is right in making his seriousness as an essential aspect of great poetry. Human existence is tragic because suffering is a permanent part of human life. But suffering is a touch-stone for human worth and a purifier of the human soul. This is why it is equated with wisdom and the nobility of the human soul. Wordsworth rightly observes, a deep suffering has humanised my soul, and the high praise bestowed on Virgil is due to his power to reveal 'the sense of tears in human things'. Aristotle is right in placing tragedy in the highest rank of the poetic forms.

Grand Style

The last quality which great poetry should possess is grand style. In his On Translating Homer Arnold defines grand style generally, though not very happily, as a style which arises when a noble mind, poetically gifted treats some great subject with simplicity or severity. He mentions Homer as the exemplar of the simple grand style and Milton of the severe grand style. But if we piece together his various references to style it will become abundantly clear that Arnold upheld the classical ideal of style which is a transparent medium for the expression of ideas, absolutely free from superfluous words and ornaments, and deliberately unobtrusive. It is a means to an end and should never be taken as an end in itself. In the essay on Wordsworth style in poetry has been compared to a pleasant in with its charms, where the traveler only halts for some time and then resumes his march towards his goal unaffected by the beauty and pleasantness of the inn. Style is a hand-maiden of ideas, not their mistress, and any tendency to overstep its modest limits is a defect, even though the offender is as great a classic of poetry as Shakespeare himself. These are the principal qualities of great poetry and the poets whose productions display them are the classics of poetry, or the poets of the front rank among the votaries of the Muses.

His Excursion is a late product when his inspiration had declined, but no serious student of Wordsworth's poetry will agree with Arnold in placing The Prelude also in the same category and describing it as the uncharacteristic product of Wordsworth's genius. As a matter of fact The Prelude or the Growth of a Poet's mind is the most characteristic and the best product of Wordsworth's Puissant imagination (to use a favourite epithet of Arnold) when the poetic fire is sustained in a long poem and philosophy and poetry are happily wedded together–a poem where Wordsworth spontaneously attains to the level of the Miltonic music and meaning without taking recourse to Milton's artifices - Latinized diction and the catalogue of the exotic proper names. The beauty which young Wordsworth loved was, by his own confession, that beauty which has terror in it, and his faith in Nature's holy plan never made him blind to the suffering which was the permanent part of human life. Nay, the homely Wordsworth is Arnold's Wordsworth, not the real Wordsworth.

A Critique on Arnold's touch-stone method

In 'The Study of Poetry' Arnold has explained the best and most effective way of testing the intrinsic quality of a poem, which is known as the touch-stone method. "Indeed", says Arnold, "there can be no more useful help for discovering what poetry belongs to the class of the truly excellent than to have always in one's minds lines and expressions of the great masters, and to apply them as a touch-stone to other poetry...when we have lodged them well in our minds. We shall find them, if we have any tact, an infallible touch-stone for detecting the presence or absence of high poetic quality, and also the degree of this quality, in all poetry which we may place beside them." Arnold then cites examples from Homer, Dante, Shakespeare and Milton. Only a couple of the examples may be reproduced to illustrate the nature of the touch-stone peculiar to Arnold.

Hamlet's dying request to Horatio:

"If thou didst ever hold me in thy heart,
Absent thee from felicity awhile,
And in this harsh world draw thy breath in pain
To tell my story."

Or take two of the Miltonic passages:

Darken'd so, yet shone
Above them all, the archangel; but his face
Deep scars of thunder had intrench'd, and care
Sat on his faded check.

Or

And courage never to submit or yield
And what is else not to be overcome.

Arnold comments that these different passages have one thing in common, the possession of the very highest poetical quality. We have acquired a sense enabling us, whatever poetry may be laid before us, to feel the degree in which a high poetical quality is present or wanting there.

Arnold's touch stone method, outlined above, raises many difficulties and cannot be accepted as a sound principle in practical criticism. In the first place, the choice of such passages is determined by a pre-conceived standard or idea of good poetry. Now the standard of one man may differ from another and so the quality of the passages chosen is bound to change complexion. Why not apply the standard direct to the poems? It will be objective, clear and intelligible. Secondly, Arnold himself has deprecated the practice of fastening upon striking fragments or single lines to the neglect of the whole poem. Arnold would probably have agreed that his method of comparing passages was not a sufficient test for determining the value of a work as a whole. He himself insisted that we must judge a poem by the total impression. But there is no reason why we should not extend his comparative method, not resting content with detached judgments from isolated passages, but comparing the whole impression that has been stamped upon our minds of one work with the whole impression that has been stamped upon our minds of one work with the whole impression that has been stamped upon our minds by a masterpiece. The comparative method is an invaluable aid to appreciation in approaching any kind of art. But if that is not enough, says Arnold, we should know that the high qualities lie both in the matter and manner of poetry, that is in the substance and the style of poetry. The matter and substance should possess, in an eminent degree truth and seriousness. The manner and style should possess a superiority of diction and movement. But observes Arnold, the truth and seriousness of matter is inseparable from the excellences of the style.

Arnold has provided us with an excellent example of how to use the comparative method. The comparative method may prove to be extremely fruitful when employed by a critic of exceptional "tact". But he seems to have underestimated the significance of the personal estimate. It is true that our personal likings and affinities may lead us to attach greater importance to a work than a more detached critic would allow. But then the fact remains that, if a piece of literature means much to us personally, it means that we have found the utmost that is really in it. It is one of the aims of the alert reader to acquire a sense of intimate personal relationship with a work of art. It may even be argued that no judgment about a book has become a real judgment until it has become a personal one. It was for this very reason that Sainte-Beuve wanted to know all about the life and circumstances of a writer before forming an estimate of his work.

Arnold seems to go too far insisting all the time on work of the highest excellence in literature. It is not fair to demand that "all hills should be Alps". There may be an excellence in some minor poetry worth while on its own account. Arnold declared that it would be much better to disregard the mass of current literature. He may be, and is right so far as permanent literary values are concerned. But contemporary literature may have a value for us precisely because it is contemporary, because it is written for us and faces our problems. By disregarding current literature completely, we shall be out of touch with the quickening forces of our time. Besides, it is just in regard to this current literature that a true critical faculty is most needed. The established classic needs no support. But the critic has a duty to perform to the promising young writers and to known contemporaries who have not got their due; and another duty to those who have been pushed into undue prominence.

Arnold did a service to criticism by his sheer exactingness. In his war against deception, insincerity, charlatanism he was relentless. "In poetry, it is the glory, the eternal honour that charlatanism shall find no entrance", he declared.

According to Prof. Garrod, this method consists in selling poetry by the pound. The conditions of the age in which writers write are different, and so are their motivations. Hence one work of art cannot be judged on the basis of the excellence of the other. Then how should one select touch stone lines selected by Arnold as the best lines of a poet, may not be treated as the best lines by some other critic. Hence Arnold's touchstone method is far from being safe or scientific.

– 3 –

A Critiquing of Arnold's 'The Study of Poetry'

Matthew Arnold (1822-1888), the Victorian poet and critic, was 'the first modern critic', and could be called 'the critic's critic', being a champion not only of great poetry, but is known and thought in world, to create a current of true and fresh ideas', and he has influenced a whole school of critics including new critics such as T.S. Eliot, F.R. Leavis and Allen Tate. He was the founder of the sociological school of criticism, and through his touch stone method introduced scientific objectivity to critical evaluation by providing comparison and analysis as the two primary tools of criticism.

T.S. Eliot praised Arnold's objective approach to critical evaluation, particularly his tools of comparison and analysis, and Allen Tate in his essay Tension in Poetry imitates Arnold's touch stone method to discover 'tension', or the proper balance between connotation and denotation in poetry.

Before Arnold a literary critic cared only for the beauties and defects of works of art, but Arnold the critic chose to be the educator. and guardian of public opinion and propagator of the best ideas.

Scott James, comparing him to Aristotle, says that where Aristotle analyses the work of art, Arnold analyses the role of the critic. The one gives us the principles which govern the making of a poem, the other the principles by which the best poems should be selected and made known. Aristotle's critic owes allegiance to the artist, but Arnold's critic has a duty to society.

To Arnold poetry itself was the criticism of life: 'the criticism of life under the conditions fixed for such criticism by the laws of poetic truth and poetic beauty', and in his seminal essay 'The Study of Poetry' 1888 he says that poetry alone can be our sustenance and stay in an era where religious beliefs are fast losing their hold, he claims that poetry is superior to philosophy, science, and religion. Religion attaches its emotion to ideas and ideas are infallible. And science, in his view is incomplete without poetry. He endorses Wordsworth's view that 'poetry is the impassioned expression which is in the countenance of all Science, adding what is a countenance without its expression?' and calls 'poetry the breath and finer spirit of knowledge'.

As a critic Arnold is essentially a moralist, and has very definite ideas about what poetry should and should not be. A poetry of revolt against moral ideas, he says, is a poetry of revolt against life, and a poetry of indifference to moral ideas is a poetry of indifference to life.

Arnold took up Aristotle's view, asserting that true greatness in poetry is given by the truth and seriousness of its subject matter, and by the high diction and movement in its style and manner, and although indebted to Joshua Reynolds for the expression 'grand style'.

In The Study of Poetry, 1888 which opens his essays in criticism: second series, in support of his plea for nobility in poetry, Arnold recalls Sainte-Beuve's reply to Napoleon, when latter said that charlatanism is found in everything. Sainte-Beuve replied that charlatanism might be found everywhere else, but not in the field of poetry, because in poetry the distinction between sound and unsound, or only half-sound, truth and untruth, or only half-truth, between the excellent and the inferior, is of paramount importance.

For Arnold there is no place for charlatanism in poetry. To him poetry is the criticism of life, governed by the laws of poetic truth and poetic beauty. It is in the criticism of life that the spirit of our race will find its stay and consolation. The extent to which the spirit of mankind finds its stay and consolation is proportional to the power of a poem's criticism of life, and the power of the criticism of life is in direct proportion to the extent to which the poem is genuine and free from charlatanism.

In *The Study of Poetry* he also cautions the critic that in forming a genuine and disinterested estimate of the poet under consideration he should not be influenced by historical or personal judgments, historical judgments being fallacious when we are biased towards a contemporary poet. If a poet is a 'dubious classic' let us shift him; if he is a false classic, let us explode him. But if he is real classic, if his work belongs to the class of the very best...enjoy his work.

In his sonnet on Shakespeare he says; 'others abide our question. Thou are free. We ask and ask- thou smilest and art still, out-topping knowledge'.

For all his championing of disinterestedness, Arnold was unable to practice disinterestedness in all his essays. In his essay on Shelley particularly he displayed a lamentable lack of disinterestedness. Shelley's moral views were too much for the Victorian Arnold. In his essay on Keats too Arnold failed to be disinterested. The sentimental letters of Keats to Fanny Brawne were too much for him.

Arnold sometimes became a satirist, and as a satirical critic saw things too quickly too summarily. In spite of their charm, the essays are characterized by egotism and as Tilotson says, 'the attention is directed, not on his object but on himself and his objects together'.

Arnold makes clear his disapproval of the vagaries of some of the romantic poets. Perhaps he would have agreed with Goethe, who saw Romanticism as disease and classicism as health. But of romanticism which posterity will not willingly let die, such as its humanitarianism, love of nature, love of childhood, a sense of mysticism, faith in man with all his imperfections, and faith in man's unconquerable mind.

Arnold's inordinate love of classicism made him blind to the beauty of lyricism. He ignored the importance of lyrical poems, which are subjective and which express the sentiments and the personality of the poet. Judged by Arnold's standards a large number of poets both ancient and modern are dismissed because they sang with 'profuse strains of unpremeditated art'.

It was also unfair of Arnold to compare the classical works in which figure the classical quartet, namely Achilles, Prometheus, Clytemnestra and dido with Heamann and dorothea, childe Harold, Jocelyn, and 'The Excursion'. Even the strongest advocated of Arnold would agree that it is not always profitable for poets to draw upon the past. Literature expresses the zeitgeist, the spirit of the contemporary age. Writers must choose subjects from the world of their own experience. What is ancient Greece to many of us? Historians and archaeologists are familiar with it, but the common readers delight justifiably in modern themes. To be in the company of Achilles, Prometheus, Clytemnestra and Dido is not always a pleasant experience. What a reader wants is variety, which classical mythology with all its tradition and richness cannot provide. An excessive fondness for Greek and Latin classics produces a literary diet without variety, while modern poetry and drama have branched out in innumerable directions.

As we have seen, as a classicist Arnold upheld the supreme importance of the architectonic faculty, and then later shifted his ground. In the lectures on translating homer, on the study of Celtic literature, and the study of poetry, he himself tested the greatness of poetry by single lines. Arnold the classicist presumably realized towards the end of his life that classicism was not the last word in literature.

Arnold's lack of historic sense was another major failing. While he spoke authoritatively on his own century, he was sometimes groping in the dark in his assessment of earlier centuries. He used to speak at times as if ex cathedra, and this pontifical solemnity vitiated his criticism.

As we have seen later critics praise Arnold, but it is only a qualified praise. Oliver Elton calls him a 'bad great critic'. T.S. Eliot said that Arnold is a 'Propagandist and not a crater of ideas'. According to Walter Raleigh, Arnold's method is like that of a man who took a brick to the market to give the buyers an impression of the building.

In spite of his faults, Arnolds' position as an eminent critic is secure. Doughlas bush says that the breadth and depth of Arnolds influence cannot be measured or even guessed at because form his own time onward, so much of his thought and outlook became part of the general educated consciousness. He was one of those critics who, as Eliot said arrive form time to time to set the literary house in order. Eliot named Dryden, Johnson and Arnold as some of the greatest critics of the English language.

Arnold united active independent insight with the authority of the humanistic tradition. He carried on, in his more sophisticated way the renaissance humanistic faith in good letters as the teachers of wisdom, and in the virtue of great literature, and above all, great poetry. He saw poetry as a supremely illuminating, animating, and fortifying aid in the difficult endeavour to become or remain fully human.

Arnold's method of criticism is comparative. Steeped in classical poetry and thoroughly acquainted with continental literature, he compares English literature to French and German literature, adopting the disinterested approach he had learnt from Sainte-Beuve.

– 4 –

Matthew Arnold As a Critic Non-Pareil

"For acute Sensitive, inspired and inspiring remarks on the man, or the work or this and that part of the work and man-attractively expressed, ingeniously co-ordinated, and redeemed from mere desultoriness by the constant presence of the general critical creed–no critic is his superior."

This is what Professor Saintsbury writes of Matthew Arnold in his *History of Criticism,* and the observation will be found highly apposite, if only we glance over the pages of Arnold's delightful Essays in Criticism which is, as Herbert Paul justly remarks, "one of the indispensable books."-," Not to have read it is to be ignorant of a great intellectual event." - "Its appearance, in 1865," says Professor Jones, "was something of a literary sensation, by reason of its style, the novelty and confidence of its opinions and the wide and curious range of its subjects." It struck a note of challenge to all the popular critics *of the day.*

But the *Essays in Criticism* cannot be fully understood and appreciated, if they are regarded as a mere collection of discourses upon various occasions and inspired by various subjects. They are a manifesto, an attempt to define and illustrate in practice, the vital functions of criticism. The first essay supplies the general critical code, which is expanded, diversified, and applied in the succeeding essays. Shortly after the Essays appeared,

Matthew Arnold wrote a letter to his sister, in which he states the motive of the book. "I have conviction," he writes, "that there is a real, and an almost imminent danger of England losing immeasurably in all ways, declining into a sort of greater Holland, for want of what I must still call ideas, for want of perceiving how the world is going and preparing herself accordingly." It was with this aim, to arrest what he conceived to be the national decay, to cure the great vice of English intellect, namely, that it is fantastic and wants sanity, to lead English literature into the paths of health and wisdom, that Matthew Arnold assumed the role of a critic and wrote the *Essays in Criticism.* In order that a national literature may be saved, it is necessary, he believed, that it must generate a sound and enlightened criticism. To him the critic seemed, indeed, to be the saviour of not only literature but also of society.

The *Essays in Criticism* did a valuable service to the cause of literature: they extended the purport of the functions of criticism in the widest possible way. Though Arnold did not meddle with art, he extended the province of literature outside of it even more widely than did Ruskin in the province of art For years together Arnold was indeed the modest yet uncompromising Socrates of London, questioning, probing, rebuking, with ironical faithfulness, the British Philistine in-literature, in journalism, in manners, politics, and philosophy; dwelling on the want of 'ideas', the want of 'light', the want of 'culture', with a mixture of sorrow and satire.

During the middle of the nineteenth century, the literary essay of the best kind had deteriorated into the short, crisp criticism which appeared in weekly papers and which was extremely defective and inadequate in its character. It was Arnold's great merit that he did much to cure this state of things by holding up Sainte-Beuve and other French critics as examples for improvement, and by urging successfully the revival of the practice of 'introducing' editions of classics by a sound biographical and critical essay from the pen of some contemporary. And, though he was at times rather eccentric in the selection of his subjects, as in the case of the Guerins, for instance, and though he showed at times a capricious and unargued preference of this and rejection of that, he exhibited, nevertheless, a great deal of critical acuteness, a wide if not extraordinarily deep reading, an honest enthusiasm for the best things, and, above all, a fascinating rhetoric.

Arnold's point of departure as a literary critic in his conception of literature as "a criticism of life." He does not concern himself greatly with the technical side of literature, which, except in his Oxford lectures "On Translating Homer," is very much in the background. His general procedure is to, go straight to the work of an author and weigh its value as a criticism of life. In this he is guided by two cardinal principles: first, that literature must have for its foundation 'sound subject-matter', and, secondly, that such subject-matter must be treated in a mood of 'high seriousness', which, according to Aristotle, is one of the grand virtues of poetry. It must not be understood, however, that Arnold does not take into account the importance of musical diction. In fact, he lays stress on melodious metre and liquid movement as much as on sound subject-matter and high seriousness. But he believes that if there is sound subject-matter and if that subject-matter is handled in a spirit of high seriousness, the grand and melodious metre and diction will inevitably follow; for thought and language are inseparably connected with each other. To quote his own words: "The superior character of truth and seriousness, in the matter and substance of the best poetry, is inseparable from the superiority of diction and movement, marking its style and manner." Or, again, in language even stronger-"The mighty power of poetry is generally admitted. But where the soul of this power, of this power at its best, chiefly resides, very many of us fail to see. It resides chiefly in the refining and elevation wrought in us by the high and rare excellence of the great style."

So far as the general trend of Arnold's thought goes, it is hardly possible to conceive of any objection; though, when he lays undue stress on the sound subject-matter of poetry, it is important to remember that genius can ennoble the lowest Subject as the want of it will debase the highest. Could Matthew Arnold have conceded that a beautiful poem might be built upon an unpoetical subject like the Mouse? But Burns, as Arnold knew, tried his hand and achieved wonderful success. Could Matthew Arnold have acknowledged that a splendid poem might be written upon a mere writing-desk? But Boileau undertook the task and gave to the world a unique "mock-epic" in his poem of Lutrin, which means in French nothing -more than an ordinary writing-desk. Or could Matthew Arnold, again, have admitted that a poet might draw his inspiration from a subject like the Ass? But Coleridge wrote, nevertheless, a beautiful poem upon the same. Well, the fact, then, is that nothing is trifling in the hand of genius, and that importance itself becomes a bauble in that of mediocrity. It is not, therefore, the subject but the treatment which makes a piece of composition poetical in its nature. When any subject, great or small, is treated in terms of emotion and imagination, it becomes essentially poetical in its character. And when this emotional and imaginative treatment is impregnated also with the spirit of music, it becomes poetical in spirit as well as in form. However, mean the subject, it becomes a thing of beauty and a joy for ever when it undergoes this triple transmutation of poetry.

"The poet gathers fruit from every tree,
Yea, figs from thorns and grapes from thistles he,
Touched by his hand the meanest weed that grows
Towers to a lily, reddens to a rose."

In the Preface to Les Orientales, Victor Hugo states the Magna Charta of poetry with admirable force and precision. "There are in poetry," he says, "no good and no bad subjects, there are only good and bad poets. Besides, everything is a subject: everything is dependent on art; everything has the franchise in poetry, ...in the great garden of poetry there is no forbidden fruit. Space and time are the domain of the poet."

Arnold's well-known dictum about poetry as "a criticism of life" is also open to the objection that it is applicable to prose no less than to poetry. In fact, when this defect was pointed out to him, Arnold himself came to acknowledge his mistake, and in a later essay he qualified his dictum accordingly and refined poetry as "a criticism of life under the conditions fixed for such a criticism by the laws of poetic truth and poetic beauty." And, no doubt, with this qualification what Arnold says of poetry is true in a general way, although the vicious "circularity" of the formula is obvious enough, and although Professor Saintsbury justly takes objection to the use of the word "criticism," saying that "either the word is employed in some private jargon, or it has no business here."

Some people commit the mistake of imagining that "criticism of life" is Arnold's definition of poetry. Arnold, it should be born in mind, never cared in the least for definitions in the abstract, though he had an extraordinary gift of crystallising his ideas in telling and memorable phrases which by their very nature tended to become favourite catch-words. His dicta about culture and religion are only too well-known. Culture is "a study of perfection;" religion is "morality touched by emotion." But, as has already been pointed out, Arnold never cared about mere definitions. He writes himself in a vein of apparent contempt: "Critics give themselves great labour to draw out what in the abstract constitutes the character of a high quality of poetry." What he does himself, in contradistinction to such critics, is to take a few perfect lines, and to suggest that they may be applied as touchstones to other poetry. Taking some typical lines from Chaucer, Dante, Shakespeare, or Milton, Arnold says of them that "the substance and matter on the one hand, the style and manner on the other, have a mark, an accent, of high beauty, worth, and power. Bat if we are asked to define this mark and accent in the abstract, our answer must be-No, for we should thereby be darkening the question, not clearing it." It is, evident, therefore, that criticism of life" is not to be regarded as a rigid, accurate, and logical definition of poetry.

When Arnold speaks of poetry as "criticism of life," he has in mind the interpretative power of poetry, by which he does riot mean, as is so often erroneously supposed., 'the power of drawing out in black and white an explanation of the universe but the power of so dealing with things as to awaken in us a wonderfully full, new, and intimate sense of them, and of our relations with them. Now poetry shows this special power of interpretation in two ways. "It interprets," says Arnold himself, "by expressing with magical felicity the physiognomy and movement of the outer world, and it interprets by expressing, with inspired conviction, the ideas and laws of the inward world of man's moral and spiritual nature. In other words, poetry is interpretative by having natural magic in it, and by having moral profundity." And to this he adds characteristically that where both qualities are united in a poet, the moral interpretation usually ends by making itself the master.

Arnold has sometimes been blamed for his undue prediction for the ethical at the expense of the aesthetic side of poetry. And there are passages in his Essays in Criticism which seem to lend support to this charge against him. In his essay on Wordsworth, for instance, he writes that "A poetry of revolt against moral ideas is a poetry of revolt against life; a poetry of indifference towards moral ideas is a poetry of indifference towards life." To guard against the possibility of misunderstanding, it is important to emphasize here that Arnold had no narrow conception of morality: it was to him almost as wide as life itself, so that poetry which ignored moral ideas was in his eyes false to human life. When he insists that poetry must deal with moral ideas, he does not mean, as is unluckily so often erroneously imagined, that it should be didactic or given to preaching. In fact, he speaks of didactic poetry always in a vein of contempt and assigns to it a grade inferior to that of any other species of poetry, ranking it even below the ballad to whose natural beauty and naive charm Arnold, the flower of academic culture was characteristically impervious. Not to say of his predilection for didactic verse, he goes even to the length of denying it the name of poetry, though, of course, he admits that it may be valuable at times from the biographical point of view. In his essay, The Study of Poetry, for example, he writes:

> *"Some kinds of poetry are in themselves lower kinds than others. The ballad kind is a lower kind; the didactic kind, still more, is a lower kind. Poetry of this latter sort counts sometimes by its biographical interest partly, not by its poetical interest pure and simple."*

He dismisses certain passages of Burns as unpoetical, saying that in them the poet is more or less preaching and not speaking from the inmost depths of his soul; while, on the -other hand, he finds The Jolly Beggars 'a piece of superb poetic success', though he admits that there is in it not only hideousness and squalor, but even bestiality. Again, he hammers hard the false idolaters of Wordsworth, who praise him because, as they say, his "ethical system is as distinctive and capable of exposition as Bishop Butler's." Even in the face of such conclusive evidence critics persist in accusing Arnold of ethical bias in his estimates of poets and poetry; but the critics are wonderful beings and their ways past finding out.

When Arnold says, therefore, that poetry must deal with moral ideas, he should not be misunderstood as saying that poetry must be didactic or that it should be given to preaching. "A large sense," he says, "is to be given to the term 'moral.' Whatever bears upon the question, 'how to live', comes under it." Arnold means that poetry must deal with life and deal with it powerfully and in that mood of high seriousness which comes from absolute sincerity, so that poetry is a voice from the inmost depths of the soul and not mere preaching conceived and composed in the mind or the head or the brain; so that poetry is nothing less than "the most perfect speech of man, that in which he comes nearest to being able to utter the truth."

Little fault can be found with Arnold's standards and ideals as a critic of poetry, though some of his methods lie open to easy and serious objection. Their defects, however, are inherent in the very qualities that give charm and individuality to the best of his literary criticisms. It is worth while here to remember that many of our misunderstandings concerning Arnold as a critic are due to the fact that he had a curious habit of emphasising one thing at one time at the cost of others equally important, so that the inexperienced reader is likely to imagine that those others are ignored by him; whereas the truth is that he emphasises those others also with equal force when their turn comes. A good many of our erroneous notions about him vanish, therefore, when we study with close attention the whole body of Arnold's literary criticism, which, with the exception of a few scattered essays, is to be found in the lectures On Translating Homer and The Study of Celtic Literature, and in the two volumes entitled Essays in Criticism. His lectures On Translating Homer constitute an admirable piece of criticism, subtle in its analysis of, and profound in its insight into, the special qualities of Homer-his eminent rapidity; his plain, forceful and straightforward directness, both in the substance of his thought and his expression; his grand style, the outcome of his nobility, simplicity or austerity, and his high seriousness-while the application of these to the translations of Chapman, Pope, Cowper, and others is full of detailed instruction. In spite of the rather strange conclusion that the best medium for Homeric translation is the English hexameter, these lectures are, indeed, a splendid piece of criticism. Nor need we be surprised at it, knowing, as we do, that Arnold had studied Homer well, had felt the characteristic qualities of his genius, and had also acquainted himself thoroughly with his English translators. The lectures "On the Study of Celtic Literature" form a work which is a veritable miracle of criticism, being, as it is, "a triumph of the intuitional method in its instinctive seizure of the things that really matter in Celtic literature, and in its picturesque diagnosis of the Celtic genius." Though Arnold had no knowledge of a single Celtic tongue and had, in consequence, to rely upon the learning of others, and though also his intuitional process has its dangers which are amply manifest in his rather uncertain and adventurous task of tracing the Celtic note in some of the English poets, his generalisations are, nevertheless, simply brilliant.

Arnold defined criticism as "a disinterested endeavour to learn and propagate the best that is known and thought in the world." The first principle of criticism is, according to Matthew Arnold, 'disinterestedness;' which is to be attained by "keeping aloof in practice," by a free play of the mind, and by the avoidance of ulterior considerations, political, social, or religious. With this goes 'knowledge;' so that no English critic, he believes, is adequately equipped who does not "possess one great literature, at least, besides his own." The next important principle is that criticism is concerned with the task of learning and propagating the best that is known and thought the best, not from the standpoint of a personal estimate, or from that of the historical estimate, but from the standpoint of genuine intrinsic excellence, unprejudiced by considerations of personal likes and dislikes, or by those of place and time.

"I wish," he says, "to decide nothing as of my own authority; the great art of criticism is to get oneself out of the way and to let humanity decide." From first to last, Arnold adhered firmly to the cosmopolitan point of view in criticism, fastening his attention upon the best and highest things in literature, and drawing also the reader's attention to them with imperturbable iteration. Now and then, of course, though very seldom, he missed his mark, as in the case of Shelley, and sometimes perhaps overshot it, as in the case of Wordsworth; but, on the whole, it must be acknowledged that he was extraordinarily quick to discern the best and highest things in literature, and that be was so confident indeed in his judgment that he cared little to reason about them, or to analyse the causes of their greatness. His criticism advocates by precept as well as by example the wide and luminous view of his great master, Goethe, and is thus a noble antidote to parochialism. It must, however, be borne in mind in this connection that every literature is attached to the life of its native soil by a myriad of invisible threads, by a thousand delicacies and implications, by many flavors, racy of the soil, which can only be imperfectly understood from the cosmopolitan point of view.

There are people who find fault with Matthew Arnold on the score of his occasional abstaining from minute analysis into the rationale of his judgment on this or that writer. The charge is unfounded; for men who have eyes to see will find that he could give subtle reasons for his opinions whenever he had a mind to do so. Not only that : he could do what is rare among critics; for he could also show that they were sometimes more than mere opinions, that they were the deliberate judgments of a trained intelligence working upon a systematic order of ideas. Nor should we be worth with him, if at times he does not dissect his judgment into all the various intellectual elements that go to make up its being. On the other hand, unless, indeed, we are willing to be spoon-fed like sickly children or like imbecile old men, it should be counted to his credit inasmuch as it sets us a thinking on our own independent account, enabling us thus to develop the critical faculty lying dormant in us. Arnold's great merit as a critic lies, indeed, not in this or that isolated opinion expressed by him but in the fact that he does not merely criticise books himself, but that, what is far more important, he teaches others how to criticise them; so that Herbert Paul is quite just when he remarks that "nobody after reading Essays in Criticism has any excuse for not being a critic."

Arnold had his critical limitations. He excluded too much. He was at times dogmatic in his judgments and capricious in the selection of his subjects. He laid all the stress of his teaching on sound subject-matter and on construction in poetry and sallies of wit and imagination pleased him not at all. His critical standpoint was cosmopolitan to a fault, so that differences of language, of aim, and of circumstances were almost altogether ignored. He believed in authority as an engine of practical good and in an academy as a means of literary salvation, forgetting that "The genius of poetry must work out its own salvation in a man. It cannot be matured by law and precept, but by sensation and watchfulness in itself." He was too fond of speaking as if there were a saving grace in method. He cared only to judge deeds as deeds, and poems as poems; he was quite incurious about men. In his critical essays he presents us with many sound rules and many memorable sentences. But in spite of all these limitations one can hardly over praise his critical work. It is wonderfully full, suggestive, and illuminating. It is lucid, sympathetic, and just. 'It is not only penetrating but also brilliant; not only conscientious but also imaginative.' Though Arnold recognised, besides the old Greeks, Goethe and Sainte - Beuve as his chief masters, "few critics have been so thoroughly original, and still fewer have had so large a share of the 'daemonic' faculty, the faculty which awakens intelligent enthusiasm in others." He struck a new note in criticism. What he did and what every other English critic before him had missed doing, was, as Sir Arthur Quiller-Couch puts it, "to treat criticism as a deliberate disinterested Art, with laws and methods of its own, a proper temper, and certain standards and touchstones of right taste by which the quality of any writing as literature can be tested: and to lay down these lines at a moment when the practitioners of criticism most needed them." The peculiar qualities of Matthew Arnold as a critic are indicated with fine discrimination by Professor Saintsbury in the following passage:-

"He had not the sublime and new inspired inconsistency of Dryden. He had not the robustness of Johnson; the supreme critical 'reason' (as against understanding) of Coleridge; scarcely the exquisite, if fitful, appreciation of Lamb, or the full-blooded and passionate appreciation of Hazlitt. But he had an exacter knowledge than Dryden's; the fineness of his judgment shows finer beside Johnson's bluntness; he could not wool-gather like Coleridge; His range was far wider than Lamb's; his scholarship and his delicacy alike gave him an advantage over Hazlitt." "Systematic without being hidebound; well-read without pedantry, delicate and subtle without weakness or dilettantism; catholic without eclecticism; enthusiastic without indiscriminateness''- Matthew Arnold ''is one of the best and most precious of critics.'' Mention must also be made of the exquisite style of Matthew Arnold. In the adoption of a ''sinuous, easy, unpolemical'' style which presents a striking contrast to the ''high-charged articles of the English newspaper critics of his day, Arnold seems to have been influenced largely by the great French critic Renan. Nevertheless, it is true, as professor Saintsbury maintains that his style cannot be assigned to any single original, being ''a sort of compound or eclectic outcome of the old Oxford academic style, as it may be seen at times in Newman, of French persiflage, and of some elements peculiar to Mr. Arnold himself.''

''The needful qualities for a fit prose,'' says Arnold in The Study of Poetry, ''are regularity, uniformity, precision, balance.'' All these qualities are abundantly manifest in his own prose, which is characterised, besides, by ease, lucidity, clearness, and a grave rhythmical movement. Arnold had the gift of condensing his meaning into striking and epigrammatic phrases which, instinct with novel charm, ran the round of literary fame and were pronounced trippingly on the tongue by every man till they became common property of every babbler of the day. Nothing exceeds the easy grace of Arnold's prose at its best. It has the lucid gleam of the morning dew and the liquid clearness of the limpid stream that runs glittering in open sunshine. No eddies, no whirlpools, no froth, no foam, its pace is tranquil and yet cheerful, bright, and free

''A dancing shape, an image gay, To haunt, to startle, and waylay.''

Though, as a rule, Arnold writes about plain things in a plain manner, he rises occasionally to a high pitch of excellence. His celebrated address to Oxford is an instance in point. Few passages of English prose are more memorable than this impressive, high-strung apostrophe to the "home of lost causes, and forsaken beliefs, and unpopular names, and impossible loyalties."

But one must be on one's guard against supposing that the style of Arnold is flawless. It is occasionally marred by the vice of repetition and of irritating mannerism. "It would have been well," says Herbert Paul justly, "if he had applied the critical pruning-knife to the exuberant mannerism which sometimes disfigures his style." Matthew Arnold is one of the best masters of "lucid, colloquial prose, plain in texture, but harmonious in cadence and scholarly in tone; and his wit, irony, satire, and never-failing urbanity combine to give an additional charm to his treatment of everything he touches.

Examples of Arnold's ironic wit may be easily multiplied, but a single illustration should be sufficient here. It is taken from his essay on Shelley in which Professor Dowden is being constantly ridiculed. This is what he writes "In one respect Professor Dowden resembles Providence his ways are inscrutable." How witty, how ironic, and yet how urbane Old Nestor might well open his lips in laughter.

To the manifold qualities of regularity, uniformity, precision, and balance; of ease, elegance, lucidity, and a grave rhythmical movement; of wit, irony, strength, and urbanity, which we have noted in Arnold, we should also add the crowning fact that his is an unmistakably individual style,–a style which, in spite of its obvious mannerisms and occasional affectations, is extremely difficult of imitation-a style the effect of which, like that of the best music, can be felt but never adequately described. No wonder, then, that Matthew Arnold, a poet of considerable eminence, was also an original force in the sister-harmony of prose; and though thrice statelier names decay, his own can wither not away

"And with those few he shall survive Who seem not to compete or strive Yet with the foremost still arrive,

Prevailing still :

The Elect-with whom the stars connive To work their will."

The great exordium of his essay on The Study of Poetry is the finest statement that has ever been made of the place of poetry in any scheme of human spiritual self-realization. He anticipates in this I. A. Richards's view of the saving power of poetry involved in its capacity to mould our aesthetic responses and impulses, and Leavis's emphatic conviction of the moral role of literature in any scheme of civilization. Of course, Arnold as a good Aristotelian could hardly be expected to ignore the cathartic qualities of aesthetic experience. But what is notable is that in speaking of the saving power of poetry he stressed the importance of conformity to the laws of poetic beauty and poetic truth. A shallow or heavy didacticism would just kill the poetry and crush the reader's aesthetic sensibility. In pleading for a large, generous disinterestedness and in his horror of vulgarity in thought and conduct he anticipates Pater. In his finely blended classicism and humanism, he is, without being a professional scholar or expositor of literature, a forerunner of the modern scholarly tradition represented by Garrod and C.S. Lewis. In his recognition of the vitality and value of the cultural tradition and aesthetic heritage of civilized Europe as the background and measure of new aesthetic achievement he is not merely a pioneer of T.S. Eliot and others who were sensitively responsive to European influences but a timeless representative of all those who recognize the irresponsible irrelevance of insularity in the sphere of art.